Dear K

Can you believe

it's finally here?

Love you honey!

Enjoy

XOXO

Cheers

Beth Dunn

Social Climbers

A Novel

By
Beth Dunn

Illustrated by Erika Whitters

authorHOUSE®

AuthorHouse™
1663 Liberty Drive, Suite 200
Bloomington, IN 47403
www.authorhouse.com
Phone: 1-800-839-8640

First published by AuthorHouse 11/17/2008

ISBN: 978-1-4389-3352-8 (sc)
ISBN: 978-1-4389-3361-0 (hc)

Printed in the United States of America
Bloomington, Indiana

This book is printed on acid-free paper.

Table of Contents

Prelude

DICTIONARY

AT - Already There. One who has social status and need not worry.

SC - Social Climber. One who aspires to be AT and has to do a lot to get there.

NR - Nouveau Riche. One who was once an SC but now has a lot of cash and can't spend it properly.

WT - White Trash. I don't think this one needs an explanation.

MC - Middle Class.

UB - Uber-Bitch.

DLG - Daddy's Little Girl

JM - J. McLaughlin, the "It" store.

SS - Social Standing. One who has it, is an AT and does not give a fuck.

IT - having it all- beauty, thinness, style, class, marriage & Money!

Dedication

For myself, my family, friends and those I look forward to meeting

You can stand under my umbrella

Introduction

How To Climb The Main Line

I'm touched by so many people; blessed really. Having your health, children, family and friends is a privilege. My life is an honor. But I didn't get it. Can you say I was *clueless?* My biggest weakness was I was a Social Climber—everyone but me could see it. I retain everything I read, am taught and told. When I watch a movie, I study it, watch the behaviors of the characters, and try to see what motivates people. I listen well to my friends when they talk about someone, learning what is socially acceptable, trying all the while to fit in. I am not a *know-it-all*—at least not now, not anymore. Sometimes I amaze myself, feel brilliant, but only for a minute, only to be knocked off my pedestal by a bitch! I cared about what everyone thought of me, *a lot*. I wanted for nothing, had everything, but still yearned for more. I was "that" person.

I was born talking. I am social by nature. Being an only child, I begged Daddy to walk me over to play with neighbors. Crying occurred when I was left out of a birthday party. When I was old enough to ride my bike I was always out with friends. Being social is just in me. It is also an issue.

I grew up, got married and had a baby. I color-coded my china with my kitchen cabinets and granite counter top.

Then it was time to give back. I wanted my family to have advantages. I was the person that was going to give them that. I wanted my husband's business to be a success, my sons to be invited to the right schools and clubs. It's not that I wanted to push them to have a certain career, I loved them for whoever they want to be, but I wanted all doors to be open to them. Plus, I still never like to be left out. I like to feel included, well liked; popular, I guess you could say. Non-Profits need women like me who have the time to dedicate to raising money to support their cultural causes. This was a way I could work without having a job. Charity work is prestigious. I was giving back to society, being popular, making sure my family gets viewed the right way…but something was wrong. I needed the charities as much as they needed me.

Social Climbing became a game, and you had to learn the rules to get to the top. There are mean women out there. A certain competitiveness came out in me. It is like I regressed. That's where I coined "the phrase." You could say it takes one to know one. They are everywhere—hiding, lurking—out for the same thing as you. Social Climbers strive for the most money, the hugest house. They are never satisfied or happy with what they have. But I learned a lot of it was crap and women were playing the same games they played in high school, only with more sophisticated rules and clothes. The ladies had extremely distracting jewelry. I lost track of what was truly important in life. Being a busy body is annoying. It took Kitty Kimmel to help me get a clue, but I am getting way ahead of myself. First, you have to understand the battlefield we were playing on.

Chapter I

THE LANDSCAPE

The Main Line is the name used to describe a cluster of elite suburbs outside of Philadelphia. Philadelphia is one of the oldest cities in the country. Philadelphia was the first capital of The United States, so the original WASPS still live in and around Philadelphia. After all, this it where it all began. New York City is too showy for us Mayflower types; we prefer the low-key, subtle side of historic Philadelphia. The City is conservative, like Boston.

The Main Line is an elegant tree lined enclave with lots of old money and estates. The countryside was perfect for development, unlike Chicago where so many places, such as Winnetka, look like sub-divisions. The Main Line lends itself to sprawling mansions. The Main Line has subtle "for sale" signs and no colored lights at Christmas! Only white lights. The "towns," as we refer to them, are filled with chic boutiques and bistros. The Main Line boasts excellent educational establishments, a strong art community (The Barnes Foundation) and fine country clubs. We Main Liners have understated, yet impeccable manners why else would we go and send our children to etiquette class?

The name, The Main Line, sounds cuter than it is. In reality, it was named for a train line. The Pennsylvania Railroad developed a rail line along Route 30, on Lancaster Avenue between Philadelphia and Paoli. As a result, many "Main Line" towns were created. Railroad executives built hotels along the line to lure well-off Philadelphians wishing to escape the summer's heat. Soon, families wanted to extend their vacations and built homes near the train stations. As residences grew, wealthy businessmen began to relocate there, building large estates, inevitably bringing about the development of the Main Line. If you're from Philadelphia and live on the Main Line, you really think you're something and you definitely want to be going somewhere. Only, in a Benz, of course, not a train.

And it is here, along our rolling hills, where the games of being on committees and being left out are played out. Main Liners are good at this game. Let's put it this way: A top business mogul is Ron Perlman. He is from The Main Line. Most of 2006/2007 *The New York Post's* Page Six focused on a socialite, Tory Burch--again from The Main Line. Um, hello, need I say more? We get "It!" Lilly Pulitzer is supposedly "via Palm Beach." I happen to know the owner lives in Villanova, smack dab in the center of The Main Line.

The people I grew up with actually never even knew there were other desirable suburbs of Philadelphia. If you are from the Main Line, you think that it is the end all and be all. It's annoying, trust me. Chestnut Hill is nice and Bucks County is lovely, but it takes a Main Liner almost

2

20+ years to even know those areas exist. If your house is actually on the train line, it is even more exclusive because all the original estates were along the train line--The Main Line. Now the train line is called the R5. I don't think they will change the name. The Main Line vs. R5? The name R5 is not sophisticated enough. It wouldn't have the right draw.

Now that you have a flavor of the battleground we play on, I can tell you the rest of the social climbing story.

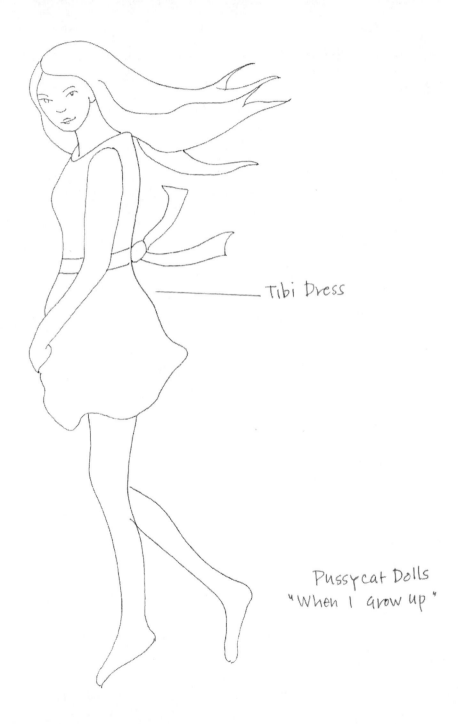

Tibi Dress

Pussycat Dolls
"When I Grow up"

Chapter II

How To Be A Socialite

"A friend is a person who knows all your faults and still
likes you in spite of them."
Author Unknown

There I was, 12 years old, using the rest room at school. I would never say "bathroom"; I was reared (as my mother always says: people rear children, farmers raise horses) to say "powder room." I heard voices and girls coming in...*great*! Sneakily, I decide to stay silent in my stall and listen. "Did you meet the new girl?" Bently Butler said to her friend. I distinctly knew her voice. We all did, as she was the most popular. We were only in the 7th grade, but already she was legacy. If your older sisters went to our school, you had a lot more credibility and respect, unless, of course, your big sister was a loser. The Butler family, however, was by no stretch full of losers. In fact, they were one of the most well-known families in town, part of a dough family legacy, and yes, money, but I mean the baking kind! I wanted to be just like her when I grow up.

"No, what's her name?" Asked another familiar voice. I think it was Kitty, a friend of mine. I stayed silent. Kitty can be mean. She was a social-climbing psychopath. Of course, I am deathly afraid of her. So Kitty was a friend of mine—get it? Neither did I… Kitty lived far away (Gywnedd), so thankfully she could only torture me at school. She literally disappeared on the weekends. I never had to see her at sleepovers or birthday parties. Kitty would say her parents were sick of driving by Friday.

"Sally," Bently said with confidence.

"That's a rather plain name," Kitty replied smugly as I sat in silence wondering where this was going. It's amazing how evil 12-year-old girls can be. But I worshipped Bentley. She was pretty, cute and funny. I wanted to be all of those things too.

"Sally Strawbridge!" I could almost see the smirk on Bently's face.

"Oh, well, that makes a big difference," Kitty said. "Where's her next class? Let's go and *please* introduce me." Kitty, like all of us, knows the Strawbridge's own a huge retail chain among many other prestigious properties on the Main Line.

That's when I first got "It." You might wonder what I mean by "It." "It" is such a vague way of explaining "It." Well, I am going to tell you. "It" begins with your name.

My friends' names are: Allegra, Colby, Mimi, and Pippa. My mother's friends are: Andi, Bunny, Muffin, and Skye. My name is Elizabeth, but I was named for Bunny. We all have a cute name. That's part of "It." I was not only named for Bunny, but I was also named for my grandmother. Your name's a really big part of "It." Your name says who you are even before you say anything about yourself or even show your face. Your name means something. People judge you by your name before they meet you. If your name is Jane Jones you better have a great personality, good clothes, and a pretty face. When you say you are named for your grandmother, to Social Climbers (SCs), that indicates that you come from an important family where one must pass on their name. So, even though Elizabeth was my grandmother's middle name, it still sounds better to say that I was named for my grandmother. My mother's name is Audrey and she is definitely an Audrey (as in Hepburn) not a Marilyn (as in Monroe). My father, Daddy, is a Third. Isn't that stately? Roman numerals are a nice addition to a name. I named my son, Greye, which is an even more fabulous name. It is also my father's middle name. "It" girls not only have the right name, but so do their offspring. Did I mention that I used to think that I was named after Queen Elizabeth because we had the same first name? Sadly, I am not related to her or even remotely related to anyone in her bloodline. However, I do have a cousin who is a professor at Oxford.

I am married. I've been married for six years and have two little boys, a five-year-old and a one-year-old, Greye and Field. Named appropriately for family names because that is what is most elegant. In fact, Greye is Fourth generation and Field is Third. SCs have their children back-to-back or it appears you can't handle it. I didn't; I could not handle it. A good SC knows you have to *love* being a mother. If four children is the new three, then I guess having two boys is like only having one. Some days it feels like I have 10 children. Oh, well!

SCs have cute names, live in cute houses--and wear cute clothes. Yet on the inside, they're not cute. Secretly, they are angry, uncomfortable, and out to get you. If you've met one, you *know*. They talk but never say anything. They make you feel ill at ease, unkempt, and unattractive. They can make you feel icky! SCs want to appear perfect. SCs want you to think they have the perfect life—the right address, neat clothes, neat nails, make perfect dinners, enroll their children in the best schools and that they have sex with their husbands every night! Yet they are hiding something. They are mean, like that bumper sticker that says (not that I would ever have a bumper sticker) "mean people suck." It does not matter where you were born, where you live or your socio-economic class, SCs are everywhere! Not just the Main Line.

I live at the New Jersey shore, a 45-minute drive from Philadelphia. I don't know how other cities, like New York City, do it. We don't have to drive three hours to The Hamptons. Philadelphians can be at the shore in under an hour. Now, Margate is not exactly a desirable year-round address. Everyone knows what the best addresses are from coast to coast. I've never been to Michigan, but I know Grosse Pointe is a desirable address. If you are from Idaho and meet someone from Darien, Connecticut, you get "It." If one vacations at the shore, that is one thing; living here is a completely different story. People always say, "You live there (big pause)… year-round?" I don't exactly "fit in" at the shore.

I live in a big house on the water. I'm married to a surgeon, not a plastic surgeon, but nonetheless, a surgeon. If you marry an investment banker or someone with the last name Vanderbilt, you know you are

"It." But people are always super-impressed that Husband is a surgeon. It shows he is smart. *The Atlantic City Press* once wrote an article, "Quinns Are to Medicine What Bushes Are to Politics." It was très sweet of the writer to compare us to the president—"W"—whom I LOVE! (Of course, we are Republicans.) Margate is a small pond on the Main Line that article would not have been written. Husband's whole family is made up of doctors, which is even more impressive because doctors used to make a lot more money, and a good SC knows her income bracket. A talented SC can sniff an AT immediately. It's a gift that they take very seriously. Then there are the NR. They are a cross in-between. They were SCs but are now ATs. They haven't quite gotten the rules down yet. They can't dress the part. They *pay* to get on the boards of charities. NRs don't have SS.

"It" is also about where you grow up. I grew up at a desirable "It" address, Radnor, Pennsylvania! Even though I now live at the shore.

Izod

Habitual
White Jeans

Jack Rogers
Monogram
Sandals

Tory Burch
Tunic

"Good Breeding"

Chapter III

INVITATIONS, DARLING

For SCs, "It" is always about the invitation. Just like when I was invited to do the Cotillion. Being invited to do the Cotillion (a group of debutantes rather than just one deb--which is very NR) when you are 18 years old is the first real thing in society that you are ever invited to do (except white glove dancing class at The Merion Cricket Club--but that doesn't count because that is the dress rehearsal for being a debutante). Unless, of course, your parents took you to parties when you were younger. My mother would drag me to operettas by Gilbert and Sullivan at Longwood Gardens (lots of Dupont sightings at those events), but never parties. All that Gilbert and Sullivan actually came in handy when I was in college. My first day of music class, a prerequisite, I was able to answer a question about operettas. Thankfully, the answer was Gilbert and Sullivan. They were the only ones I ever went to. I did not even like them really. Secretly though I wanted to name dogs Gilbert and Sullivan. I thought the names were cute, but the music annoying.

Getting back to the invitation, this story *starts* with "an invitation." The invitation to be a member of a Tea Club, an exclusive group of women who attended exclusive schools on the Philadelphia Main Line. They call themselves "The Tea Group." Only 30 are asked. The people who orchestrate this tea group did so because their mothers had been in a tea group, a secret tea group (like the Skulls). Their members included all of the big names from the Philadelphia Main Line: The Hamiltons of Campbell Soup fame, Dorrences, and Wanamakers--just to name a few. I know about these people because I grew up there. I went to school with them, at The Agnes Irwin School, an all girls' school named in *The Official Preppy Handbook*. It is the school that everybody thinks of when they think of the epitome of status, and high society and, yes, it is the perfect place to study SCs. "It" girls go to the right prep schools and universities. A lot of ATs went there. SCs wish they went there or are trying to befriend groups of women that went there. The problem with SCs is they seem to fit in. They look the part. Oftentimes they are the part. Yet something deep down is making them bitter and jealous.

Once you are invited, all you can think about is an outfit. So now it is about what to wear. It's a Spring Tea in April. I locate a beautiful white, tweed suit. Chanel-like because all SCs know how to copy a look. Even if you can't afford the real thing you must appear to be wearing a designer. I'm wearing Banana Republic with yellow peep toe pumps and a matching yellow clutch—Perfect! The tea is to be held at the home of Kitty Kimmel. It's a beautiful, stately English Tudor home (six bedrooms) in Haverford, Pennsylvania, adjacent to their club. Kitty has big bushels of roses and tulips as the centerpieces in her dining room, entrance hallway, and over the fireplace and in the kitchen.

All the women arrive with flowers in their hands, the perfect hostess gift. "It" is just not how you are dressed, "It" is also what you bring. SCs are infamous for bringing a beautiful hostess gift: tulips or a bottle of wine in a toile bag. SCs act as if they like you. Many SCs design their own line of something—china, clothing, jewelry etc. So a good hostess gift to get Kitty Kimmel is your latest scarf. I secretly think SCs want to be Vera Wang but don't really feel like working that hard. Maybe their husbands won't let them work because they can't afford to hire the help needed to work that many hours. That's just one theory. *I have many.*

Tea, sandwiches and scones are served, and a society photographer is in attendance. Of course, to be photographed is the ultimate SC dream. The more pictures of you in the paper, the more important you must be. I must warn you, society photographers are SCs. They expect to be known, and they will gossip about your misfortunes. So, you try to position yourself near the photographer in hopes that he or she will take your picture, that it will be published, and that everyone will talk about you and think you are "It." "Oh, did you see Kitty Kimmel's picture in the paper?" One time Mimi Montgomery's picture was in the paper three weeks in a row. She was at three different parties but wore the same dress at all three. It was only from Nicole Miller (big mistake, as they display all their coolest designs in the window). We made fun of her. I mean, we secretly whispered behind her back for a very long time afterward. I have literally watched women chase down a society

13

photographer. **I swear!** "It" girls, of my grandmother's generation, knew that there were only three times in your life that you should ever be in the newspaper. This is what differentiates an AT from an SC. They knew that if you've truly made it you did not want to be in the paper, especially with your picture, except for your birth, your marriage and your death. That has all changed now. Colby and I call the society pages the funny pages. An SC would be happy to see her picture in the paper every week. Even though we don't live in New York City and our pictures rarely appear in *Vogue* or *Town & Country*, we still have our high society. Every town does.

Naturally, no one is really drinking tea. Everyone is pretty much drinking wine. Chardonnay is very SC. I have heard that red wine is better for your metabolism, but an SC could care less, as she would never drink red wine in public. It would stain her teeth.

Everyone is chatting. There are people who seem nice, and there are people who are standoffish, "cliquier." There is something about unfriendly, self-conscious people. I'm feeling a hot flash come over me. This is possibly the most attractive group of women I have ever seen! Quickly, I have to find a friend with whom to talk. I locate Colby. "Darling, your shoes are so cute. Where did you get them?" I ask, as I approach her. Colby and I went to Agnes Irwin together.

"The French Lemon," Colby smiles. I pull her to the side so we can really chat. "Did you see Kitty when I came in?" I ask.

"Yes, she gave me a tour of her dressing room, even the ceiling had toile wallpaper on it!" Colby smirks.

"Typical, she wants everyone to know she has a room full of Gucci shoes. I think she glared at me." I often feel Kitty glare at me, I'm not sure why. It might be all in my head. I'm insecure. Just then I spot her again. For a second I check her out, of course, especially her outfit. Kitty has long, thick blond hair, fair, ivory skin and blue eyes. She is wearing a pearl cuff bracelet and ring, diamond earrings and a short lavender dress, not really her color, but it shows off her long legs. Kitty does not have large breasts, not even a "handful," as Husband states are the perfect size. Kitty is flat-chested, but she is very slight--it works for her. She is very dainty, demure and elegant. Kitty is tall enough to look statuesque, but the heels help.

"Who cares. She's an UB," Colby quickly adds. "She's miserable. I heard she is having trouble getting the girls into Tarlton. She hired a private tutor she isn't admitting to, and can't believe she's still not able to get them in. She's probably in a bad mood." Colby says, teetering her glass of wine in one hand. "It" girls know how to hold a wine glass just so. Not holding on too tight. Their grip is loose, just the thumb and forefinger. The arm is also always relaxed and bent at the elbow. The glass becomes an extension of their hand, held up near the mouth— almost as if ones smoking it. Colby always makes me feel better. It's her job as my best friend. So, overall, the tea is fun, and I chat with Merritt and Bryn.

"Hi, Ladies," I say, air-kissing them.

"How is Field?" asks Bryn. She is so sweet.

"So cute. A monster and into everything, but very funny," I say, not wanting to complain too much. Issues with children are so not cute tea conversation. "How is your husband?" I ask Merritt, whose husband is always the life of a party. I can never remember the names of all the husbands. You meet too many people at events. It's hard enough remembering the women.

"Oh, the usual. You will see him at the Antique Show. Hopefully he will behave," Merritt smiles and rolls her eyes. *Will I?*

Instead, "How is your daughter, Bryn?" I say, keeping the conversation alive.

"She is perfect," Bryn smiles. *Of course she is.* Do I have the only difficult children? How does Mommie put it? My sons are "spirited." We continue to talk about our children and our husbands and our non-jobs and the committees that we are on. Everyone seems to discuss only her children or her husband—BORING!

"Do your children like school?" I ask Merritt. Merritt's family is big at Tarlton a prestigious private pre-school.

"Yes, they love it." Merritt has major lockjaw. So cute.

Teas are held monthly on the last Wednesday of every month promptly at 4:00 P.M. This is just like in London. I read once that the spoken English language in the United States is closest to original English but we still all wish we had a foreign accent. The next best thing is a nanny with a foreign accent. Most of the ladies host the tea in their home or a hotel, some at the Cricket Club. Sometimes Husband thinks I am in denial that I live at the shore, since I go to Philadelphia and the Main Line all the time, even to get my nails done, as they have the best salons.

Anyway, tea is very pleasant and attractive. Everyone is very traditionally dressed in bright colors. All are having a good time. You must be very careful about what you say because you don't want it to be repeated. You also don't want to sound like a gossip, be too self-centered, look like an ass, or say something rude about someone and have it get back to him or her. You definitely don't want to be the drunk girl. Conversation at the Tea Party is very calculated and contrived. In fact, most people are talking about the weather, just like in the movie "Pleasantville."

Colby and I immediately call each other the minute we leave tea. We must fully discuss everyone there, what they were wearing and what they said. "I cannot believe she showed you her closet. She is such an SC!" I practically bark as I light a cigarette. I am a social smoker. A Marlboro light after a glass of Chardonnay makes me happy.

"I know it is to show off," Colby sort of sneers.

"If I had 300 pairs of Christian Louboutins, I still wouldn't be showing anyone my closet," I spit as I exhale.

"It is really pathetic, but her house is stunningly nice," Colby says. Colby is adorable with a short blond bob. She has pretty blue eyes and is always dressed preppy-chic, with flair. Her parents are not originally from the Main Line. That's why I can stand her. Even though she grew up rich, her parents did not, so she knows better than to be a total snob. Her mother and father are from some place in the Midwest (not Shaker Heights, Ohio either), so it was hard for them to break into the Main Line clique. Now Colby has enough Hermès to be envied! Colby, smartly, does not display her Hermès boxes in her living room like a work of art, like an SC we know.

"I heard that when Pippa wasn't asked to be in the tea club she cried for two days." Pippa is NR: Even though she has the right last name *now*, my tea group is on to her. More on that later.

"Really?" Colby contemplates, "that's pathetic and sort of psychotic."

"Kitty doesn't like her," and what Kitty says goes.

"I like The Tea Group. I think it is going to be really fun," agreed. But The Tea Group can use some lightening up. There's wine after all.

"Colby, I must run, Husband is beeping in," I say. I always take Husbands calls.

"Okay, call me tomorrow," Colby says.

I say, "Love you," as I am hanging up.

"Good Vibrations," by Marky Mark plays on the radio on the way home to the shore.

It's terrible that Pippa got left out. Kitty is being mean. She's not the mayor of The Main Line. I, for one, have noticed that SCs have an extremely high, over-inflated sense of self-worth. I mean, whom do they think they are judging others? It is not as if they are Babe Paley or Sally Quinn. The problem with SCs is that they think they are all that. They don't realize that they're not!

"AT" Names:

Barrie

Beatrice

Bibby

Bif

Catherine

Claire

Coco

Cricket

Dotty

Lilly

Frances

Grace

Mackie

Jackie

Kathleen

Rose

Ruth

Scarlet

Saylor

Naming your child after your maiden name, but calling it a pet name.

Naming your daughter after yourself or your mother.

Family Names

NR/SC Names:

Ashley

Barbie

Blaine

Blaire

Bree (anyone named after a cheese except Colby)

Bisque

Chelsea

Chandler

Charlotte

Daphne

Emma

Hunter

Mercedes

Montana

Madison

Mandy

Paris

Penny

Porsche (or any car for that matter)

Sloan

Taylor

Named after a movie, TV star or singer (i.e. Brittany or Reese)

Chapter IV

DEATH BY COMMITTEE

"Hi, my little private caller," Colby says as she answers the phone. All "It" girls have private numbers. Her mother and I are the most frequent people that call her with blocked private numbers. Since her father and husband are doctors, she understands. If a patient captures your number, he will haunt you. "What are you doing?" Colby asks politely.

"Drinking my Borba water and staring at my closet," I answer despondently. I hate that nothing fits in my closet. Having nothing to wear is a huge bummer.

"What is Borba water?" Colby is clueless.

Um, hello? You add the dry powder to your drinking water and it makes your water turn blue, tastes like a piña colada, and everyone in Beverly Hills drinks it. You get it at Sephora.com.

"Detox water. You know, so I can lose weight," I educate. Toxins build up in your system and make you retain water, slowing your metabolism, and then you don't feel well. If you are going to drink wine then you better dry brush with an elemis skin brush. It's like a hairbrush but for your

21

skin. Before your shower, put elemis detox oil on your pulse points, take an elemis herbal detox bath twice a week and take whole body cleanse vitamins. I mean, come on.

"Nicki has you on the craziest routine! It's like a religion." Colby thinks I am ridiculously absorbed with my looks. She works out with Nicki too but doesn't take all her advice. Colby's not into advice.

"What are you doing later?" I ask. I need a friend to cheer my fat ass up.

"Tennis lesson, a nap, the girls' school fair meeting and then nails," Colby answers. Colby takes a nap every day. She's also a slave to her daughters' school. Colby talks baby talk around her daughters. When she has to use the powder room she says she going "potty." Colby says her favorite show is Hannah Montana; her favorite book is Dr. Seuss, favorite music—Disney.

"Perfect. I'll meet you there. I need my nails done," I say. "OMG, Colby, I have to run. Kitty is calling me," I say as I click over. "Hi, Kitty," I say answering my other line. I am slightly afraid of Kitty.

"Hey, Elizabeth, did you have fun at tea?" Kitty asks.

No. Kind of dull instead I say, "It was so fun. Thank you again for including me. I love what you did in your dining room. It looks amazing, who did it?" I say like the fake ass that I am.

"Thank you. Nicole, of course," Kitty takes a breath, " I'm calling to see if you would consider being on the Philadelphia Antique Show committee. Kit and I are the co-chairs!" Even though the women do all the work, husbands and wives always serve on all committees together. Like a team. Isn't that cute? Kit is a typical main line man. Very tall, very blond, blue eyed and blue-blooded. He's in investments of some sort, maybe mergers and acquisitions, who knows. He was on the crew team so he has very broad shoulders. Kit is the eternal frat boy, and who doesn't love a frat boy!

"Sure, I would love to, Kitty," I say, never wanting to miss a party or anything else for that matter. Plus, I'm on the committee every year.

"It's not totally fun. You're expected to work, but then you can see all the displays," Kitty adds.

I'm thinking, yeah, like I can afford anything there. "That's great, we would love to do whatever you need us to do," I say with enthusiasm. It is pathetic. Why am I so insecure?

"All the big families will be there: Drexel, Chew, Biddle. It will be great exposure for your husband," Kitty adds.

Who? Since when has Kitty ever had Husband's best interest in mind? "Perfect, it's always fun to meet new people," I say, trying not be totally disgusted with her name-dropping, or my lack of knowledge. Living at the shore makes it hard to remember all the players.

"Did you see your picture in *The Main Line Times*?" Kitty asks.

How does she keep track of all of the society pictures, I wonder. "No, is it awful?" *Ugh*, I worry, as I am carrying too much weight and don't want a bad picture in the paper for all to see. Especially ex-boyfriends.

"You look fine, you are so photogenic," Kitty says pleasantly.

WHAT? That is by far my least favorite compliment EVER. It insinuates that you are not naturally as pretty as you look in the picture. *BITCH!* "Cool, I will have to pick up a copy today," I say lightly.

"Oh, what are you doing today?" Kitty asks.

None of your business is what I want to say. "Oh, the usual, errands, dinner." *Not.* But I don't say that. She is not coming with Colby and me.

"Call me if you are around and want to get coffee. I have to pick out more fabric swatches because now we're doing the master suite," Kitty says.

Must be rough. "Will do, Kitty. I should get going, but thanks again for including me," I say, wanting to get off the phone.

"No problem," Kitty says, hanging up.

Why do I have this love/hate thing with her? More on that later.

I slather on honeysuckle and pink grapefruit lotion, my all-time new favorite for spring scent. Plus, I read that the smell of grapefruit suppresses your appetite. I put my hair back so some pieces fall in my face and I tuck them behind my ear. I look very 1960s Jackie O.

I jump into my car, inserting my Tiffany & Co. monogrammed key chain to start the engine. I actually don't really like key chains from there, they always break and you lose the little silver screw-on ball. I have received so many as gifts I still have a stash. I decide to call Mommie on my way to get my nails done. "Hi," I say as she answers.

"Hello, darling, what are you doing?" she asks in her quiet, soft way of talking.   "Nothing. Just getting my nails done," I say. "Last time I got a pedicure I used OPI "Sweetheart," and it was way too light and all wrong for a pedicure." These are the types of things we discuss at length.

"I only use "Bubblebath" by OPI in the spring," Mommie says. Mommie would be really cute, if she wasn't my mother. She is short, like me, but with blond hair. We both have matching blue eyes, violet-blue like Liz Taylor, I was once told. She is always a size 2 petite. Mommie is in perfect shape from all her skiing and gardening. She wears her hair in a French twist every day. She always has on the cutest flats I've ever seen, even when they're not in style.

"Well, my new favorite is "Limo Scene" by Essie," I add. My mother thinks she's perfect and does everything right, including the nail polish she chooses. That must be why we spell her name with an "ie" on the end. My mother could never be plain enough to spell her name Mommy.

"Oh, I haven't seen that one. Is it new?" Mommie asks.

No. "Not really. It's pretty. You should try it," I say.

"How are the boys?" Obligatory grandparent question.

"Perfect," since they are, especially when I'm not watching them. "Could you save your copy of *The Main Line Times*?" I am dreading seeing this picture.

"Yes, is your picture in it?" Mommie sounds excited. "Bunny's calling from LA. I should take this," Mommie says as she kisses goodbye.

As I pull into the gas station I see Sue Smith's Jetta. *FUCK*, I really don't want to talk to her about which summer camp Greye is going to attend. Sue's son goes to school with Greye. I really need gas, and this is the best price around. I will say even though New Jersey isn't exactly where I thought I would live, at least I don't have to pump my own gas. Jersey girls don't pump gas (another bumper sticker I will never have—but it makes me laugh). Self-serve is not offered in New Jersey—it's the law. I put my visor down and start plucking my eyebrows, willing her not to see me. The best light for plucking is in the car. Then I put my cell phone to my ear and pretend to be on it as I look forward, hoping not to catch eyes. Phew. Minutes pass and I realize I am off the hook as I glance in my rear view mirror and see her car is gone. I get so sick of talking about schooling for my children. It's nauseating. "Poor some sugar on me," by Def Leopard plays as I drive to The Main Line.

Colby walks in, looking her fabulous self. She's so well coordinated, wearing her Tori Burch brown tunic, her Trina Turk brown floral flowing skirt, her Prada kitten heel strappy sandals and her Fendi spy bag in ivory. She is too cute! "It" girls have the right wardrobe. I am already soaking and the massage chair is rubbing my ever-throbbing back and hot towels are on my shoulders and neck. "Hello," Colby smiles. Colby selects Essie nail polish "A Room with a View", a beautiful neutral color for spring. It is tacky to have color on your nails, except in the fall and February. Red is acceptable those months. As you can see I like to make up rules, and make lists. I know better now; my standards are not always appropriate.

"Hello," I say back. I have selected "Like Linen" by Essie. "Remember when we were in the Paris Ritz drinking Serendipities and each came with a fresh-cut rose?" I ask. The Hemmingway bar in The Ritz Carlton, Paris is magnificent!

"Of course." Colby is beaming at the memory of our after-college trek through Europe.

"Well, this is almost as good, sans the drink," I say, relaxing. I have the orange Tory Burch ballet flats that look so Hermès. I love that they were ¼ the price.

"Agreed," Colby says opening, *US Weekly*, the only thing she reads now that she is a mother and a self-proclaimed "too busy to pick up anything else with any kind of substance." Colby is too absorbed in her children, if I am too absorbed in my looks. Not that children shouldn't be a top priority. I love my little angel babies. I tell them they are a gift from God. I put myself first is all. Unlike those people on the Oprah show who can't say "no" or let themselves "go." I take impeccable care of myself. It can take ten minutes for me to get ready to shower. Oprah would be so proud of me.

Remember when Jackie O wrote in her college yearbook her ambition in life was "To *not* be a house wife?" Colby's was the exact opposite. All she has ever wanted to do was be a mother and a housewife. Now she is one!

"Sorry, I all but hung up on you earlier when Kitty called." Colby gives me the knowing look. Colby is on my side but thinks I need to grow up. "Kitty asked Husband and me to be on the PAS committee," I say, waiting to hear if Colby has been asked.

"Yes, we're doing that too, it should be fun," Colby says.

Not. "Let's try to have the same shift so we can have a drink afterwards," I say, knowing I will feel more secure having her by my side.

"Perfect," Colby smiles. "Kitty passed me in her car today and did not say anything or even look at me. Don't you think that's strange?" asks Colby. "Do you think she's insecure?" Colby adds.

"No, when I see someone and ignore them it's because I don't want to talk to them," I say bluntly. Thinking of poor Sue Smith. Or rather, how rude I am.

"Oh, why do you think she wouldn't want to talk to me?" Colby asks.

"Maybe she was off to one of her committee meetings. You know how important and busy she is." We both laugh.

Colby knows it is my ultimate dream to be the co-chair of opening night at the Ballet. I love ballet. I really do. I mean it. I have been doing it my whole life, and I love their bodies. They are so thin. I wish I looked like that. And I love The Nutcracker Prince. In the end of The Nutcracker, when the prince takes Clara away on his sleigh, that is the most romantic scene; it is better than any love movie or book out there. I grew up waiting for my prince to take me away. *Does taking me to New Jersey count?*

"How is Bridgett working out?" I ask Colby about her latest nanny. I wonder how many she has had so far.

"Great, I think she's doing really well," Colby answers with her nose in the gossip magazine.

I finally saw my picture in *The Main Line Times*. I look pretty. Not fat, which is a miracle. Mommie saves the pictures for her photo albums. She is so proud.

SOCIAL CLIMBING 101:

Think, or at least act, like you are better than everybody else.

Be Conceited

Be Self-Centered

Think the world revolves around you

Be Smug

Talk behind people's backs

When you are saying someone's name, mention the street they live on e.g.

"You know Kitty Kimmel she lives on Gray's Lane in Haverford."

Care excessively about what people think about you

Still wear a Lester Lanin hat.

Be Self-Righteous

Be Critical

Be Judgmental

Be Opinionated

Have monograms everywhere

Be Calculated

Be Contrived

Plot

Be Devious

Be Driven

Be Deceptive

Be Determined

Be Manipulative

Be friends with people for the benefits.

Aren't interested in Romance.

Drop friends if a better invitation comes along.

Don't look people in the eye.

Complain about what to wear.

Don't really like their Husbands.

Don't care about their children.

Complain how exhausting being on all these committees is.

Lie

Brag

Want to get ahead and will do anything to get there.

Exaggerate

Be Nosy

I do want to explain something. I am not vehemently against social climbing. I'm just vehemently against mean SCs. There's nothing wrong with wanting to further yourself or better yourself. My motto has always been: "constant state of improvement." I see that as strength, as a positive character trait. I can be a total SC, just a nice one.

SCs are different. They are not trying to be smarter or better people or improve themselves or their families. They are out for number one, and they are evil about it. An AT has SS. With SS comes respect, and then you have everything. SCs are hiding something. They are vulnerable. It's as if they don't want to be found out, or are ashamed. Every day it is a feat in "getting away with it." "It" is all about perception.

I've noticed SCs marry for money. The rest of us fall in love in our teens or early twenties. If the father of our loves is a success, that is the only measuring tool. SCs just marry the father. It looks good on paper, so why not. After all, the father already owns the company, so your SS is secured. Husbands are huge accessories to SCs. I don't actually think SCs like their husbands. But if the Husband went to a good school/schools, or knows someone important, or has multiple club memberships, or a trust fund, then they are worth marrying and bragging about. At the end of the day, no real SC likes their husband, but they are a vital accessory.

Children are another accessory for SCs. Main Liners are married and stay at home with their children. They do not work. The way they name their child, dress their child, and the abilities their children have and the music class they attend are all used to social climb. If your child is in school (French class, reading class, gym class et al) with someone else's child, whose family you want to know this is a good opportunity for SCs. Even if your children are not friends or get along, SCs will try for play dates so as to befriend the "It" couple. Playgroups are another huge SC outlet. Having the appropriate accessories is necessary. For example, I have the Maclaren stroller (SCs use the term coach or pram vs. stroller)—Burberry edition—with the matching diaper bag. They both have the plaid lining with black piping. One time, I mispronounced Maclaren, but Colby quickly corrected me. The baby's room is decorated in a Scalamandre fabric with matching wallpaper. You can't have a play date with an "It" couple if your stuff isn't socially acceptable. All of our sons' clothes are from the Children's Boutique;

custom roll neck monogrammed sweaters, knits in cashmere for the layette, especially Ralph Lauren or Marcella Saret (a.k.a France), and then clothes from Bon Point; very distinguished. A custom baby basket was designed for both sons at Saks Fifth Avenue. A SC will overdress her children, as if they are little dolls. When a five-year-old male child is wearing a linen jumper with a Peter Pan collar, you have an SC on your hands. By the way, all SCs have C-sections. They would never dream of ruining their body in childbirth. Again, they lie, "I pushed for hours, but they had to give me a C-section," or "my hips are too narrow, and the baby was just too big." In reality, it's, "I did not want to gain the last few bloating pounds, so I scheduled a C."

SCs have their children's color charts done so that they maximize their looks by dressing them in their best colors. Once you know your child's palette, you know what color clothes to buy so they can always look their cutest. (Greye looks good in brown; it matches his complexion. Field looks good in blue; it matches his eyes.)

What exactly is an SC? An SC is definitely attractive with a cute name that they might have changed. Beware of the SC that was known by one name in high school but when they went to college and joined a sorority, they changed their name completely. So, when you are back on Cape Cod for the summer and play the name game, this person's name no longer exists because they changed it. That is a really deep-rooted SC. They are popular but they are sort of vindictive. SCs have a look in their eye. A lot of SCs are from out of town, and they over-exaggerate the Main Line look. Trust me, some SCs are not from out of town though. Out of town SCs are pretty scary. They're wearing Nantucket red shorts, an izod with collar up and a navy blue blazer with a signet ring, or everything that matches from the bow in their hair to the bow on their shoes, (to their dress, to their Bermuda bag). It is all too much and they are trying to be hip, but you can see they are trying too hard. SCs prey on your weaknesses. SCs want you to talk about yourself, but they keep their own life bottled up. For example, they would never admit that they get chemical peels or drink Penta water (which has more oxygen and is better for hydration). They do not want to share any of those things, or any of their secrets--good or bad. If they score a bag that looks Louis Vuitton, and you compliment it, they will never tell you where they go it. If they have a beautiful Chloé outfit on major sale they will never admit it. SCs have the ability to change the subject quickly and also not answer direct questions.

The other thing I want to mention about the Main Line is that it isn't like Park Avenue. It's not that swell. It's not that perfect. These women—the SCs—come in all different shapes and colors. I can definitely categorize certain of their attributes, but everyone looks different, has her own distinct personality, way of dressing, way of looking. And all of us here don't live in a science-fiction movie, like "The Stepford Wives." Not everyone is pencil-thin. Not even the SCs!

If you grow up on the Main Line, there are only four acceptable schools: The Agnes Irwin School, The Haverford School, Episcopal Academy and The Baldwin School. If you went to Boarding School (that's the ultimate), make sure it was someplace like Foxcroft, Dana Hall, or Woodberry Forest. If you went to Proctor, don't brag as that is a school everyone goes to when they have been kicked out of two others.

All SCs belong to a couple of different non-profit clubs besides being on committees. To belong to the Junior League and the DAR (Daughters of the American Revolution), it is extremely prestigious. First City Troop for the men.

Also, there are three social/country clubs that are acceptable for membership. When the Main Line began there was The Golf Club a.k.a. Merion Golf, The Cricket Club a.k.a The Merion Cricket Club and The Country Club a.k.a Philadelphia Country Club. If you don't belong to one of them, you might as well forget it.

SCs must have their hair blown out. Getting regular manicures and pedicures are as important as diamond rings and pearl earrings. I received a questionnaire once that asked, which do you prefer, diamond or pearls? I replied, both! As if I could pick one or the other. During the winter, the nail polish is typically Essie "Mademoiselle." In the summer, we add a layer of "Ballet Slippers" from Essie to a layer of "Mademoiselle." That gives a little more pink and really supports your summer Lily Pulitzer outfits. I know the buffed non-polished nails are so in, but I look better in nail polish. Plus, we are always a bit behind the times and trends here in Philadelphia. We have a few years to catch up.

There are two types of SCs. The first is the one that is relatively quiet but friendly. They are self-conscious, somewhat on the introverted side. Once you get talking to them however, you think they are friendly. You think that you had a nice conversation with them. It is not until later that you find out they made fun of your shoes. The other type of SC is outgoing and very friendly. They are talkative, polite, and interested. They ask you a lot of questions about yourself. **Beware!** This is often a sign that they are quizzing you to see how you answer and to figure you out to see if you are worth it. Once again, you find out later that they said something nasty about your shoes. SCs also say rude things to your face. I hate this trait most because I am never quick enough to retort. I usually don't even realize until later that I was insulted, or I just stand there, dumbfounded. You see, SCs are smart. They keep their friends close and their enemies closer.

You may wonder why everyone is climbing and where they are climbing. Well, we can't all be Princess Charlotte of Monaco or Princess Madeline of Stockholm, and we can't all marry Prince William. Nevertheless, we're all going to die trying. Social climbing is not always necessarily a bad thing. One has to social climb in order to elevate oneself or to get ahead. That can be good. It's important to strive and have ambition. I believe people should be less calculated about it and be a little bit more polite. After all, we all must live in this world, and I think there should be some rules. It's like the Sinatra song says, "let's leave the party polite." Doesn't anyone have anything better to think about than what committee they are on?

SOCIAL CLIMBERS:

Drink Chardonnay

Name Drop

Pass Judgment

Pose for pictures in the paper

Are Cunning & Shallow

Name their homes

Are Fake

Gossip

Play Tennis, irrelevant to weather or not they are good

Hide things

Are emotional wrecks

Are always on their cell phone

Act like they're your best friend and then tell everyone your secrets

Closet smoke, drink--you name it

Belong to Country Clubs (and think it is really cool)

Were cheerleaders (and thought that was cool)

Put Chanel tags in INC suits-(please, designer! I think not.)

Claim to be wearing Michael Kors but it is his Macy's line

Correct people when they mispronounce their SC name or spelling

Sign all correspondences xoxo

Think Kate Spade purses are cool

Try to intimidate

Pretend their dress and shoe size is a size 6, even if it is not

Talbots glasses

Cashmere sweater

Lacoste tennis shirt

Jennifer Miller Jewelry

also Lacoste

K Swiss

37

SOCIAL CLIMBERS SIGNATURE TRAITS:

Blond Hair

Unique Names/ Unique spelling to a name

Ulterior Motives

Tiffany's engraved key chains

Volvo Station Wagons

Lock Jaw

Skeletons in their Closets

Memorize The New York Times Style Section

Monogram: car, placemats, soap, napkins, silverware, towels, linens,
glasses, stationary, jewelry, pillow cases, socks, toilet paper et al.
(Especially if they married up and want to show off there new name!)

Back Stab

Cartier Tank Watches

Pure breeds for pets

No eye contact

Van Cleef & Arpels

Pratesi

Aqua Di Parma

Animals as decorations

Super matching DVF luggage

Pretend they have had sex with only 3 people in their entire life

Super matchy desk sets by Ballard Designs

Know every fashion designer/ brand/ jewelry by heart

Hire professional photographers for Christmas cards

Molton Brown

Hire publicists, and never admit to it

Chapter V

How To Be A Co-chair

Another invitation arrives. "Hello, Mrs. Quinn," my mailman says to me with a shit-eating grin. He can't help but notice that for Margate, Mrs. Quinn seems to get the most elegant envelopes and the glossiest, largest magazines he has ever seen. I do have impeccable taste.

"Good morning," I say, a bit embarrassed, as I'm still in my silk pajamas. I have to admit, I love to admire all of my fancy invitations hanging in my kitchen. I immediately rip open the envelope! It is an invitation to be on the Committee for the Academy Ball, the ultimate, annual, social gala held in Philadelphia Society. At the age of thirty-two, what more can you possibly want? If you've been a debutante, been engaged, had the proper wedding and then are asked to be in "The" Tea Group and now to be on the Committee for the Academy Ball, it's overwhelming, exciting and again, "It" is all about the invitation.

The Academy Ball is the who's-who of Philadelphia Society. They have a "program book" which is more like a yearbook. Rich people buy pages supposedly for charity but the pictures are of Philadelphia

Socialites playing tennis, golf or sailing on their yachts in ball gowns and wearing fancy jewelry. If you cannot attend The Academy Ball, unlike other charity fundraisers, one still rsvp's and makes a donation to the committee for fear of not being invited back. *Can you imagine? Sort of sad.* It is the most expensive party in Philadelphia. And "It" is fabulous!

SCs have a mental checklist in their heads when they turn twenty-two. You know what you need to do. It's what you remember from growing up on the Philadelphia Main Line. "It" is what you must do. Number one: You *must* join the Junior League—that's no problem. Mommie was a member of the Junior League, and so I had no trouble getting in to it. Number two: You *must* get married. Obviously, you want to be the first one to get married, and the first one to have children. It's revenge. Number three: You *must* be asked to be in the Tea Club. Number four: You *must* be on several committees. The most prestigious are the Philadelphia Museum of Art, the Philadelphia Academy of Fine Arts (PAFA) and the Philadelphia Academy of Music. Once you reach there, it's like there is nowhere else to go, at least in Philadelphia. For each of these you receive an invitation.

"It" girls get/send out the best invitations and monogrammed stationary. SCs try to send the best invitations. Whether it's a wedding invitation or a shower invitation, they use ivory card stock from Cranes, the same stock that Cartier and Tiffany and all the big names use. If it is a tea invitation, they have selected a pretty card with a floral bouquet or a little teacup or a frog. Invitations set the tone. And they are the most important part of life, the most important part of the party. What did that one important person say? "It's all about showing up." Well, you can't show up if you don't receive the perfect invitation.

I remember my first invitation. It was the first one I ever designed myself. It was for my Sweet Sixteen, inviting 150 of my closest friends at the Willows. The invitation was a thick white card and in the windowpane was hot pink script. I don't remember my invitations from my birthday parties when I was a little girl anymore, but things have certainly changed. Now, for a birthday party, parents ask whether their child should wear play or party clothes? *What?* People are really unbelievable! We just played games and won prizes; now parents hire staging crews and event planners. Honestly, what is this world coming to? I heard that Kitty hired a graphic art designer for the tea invite. The graphic artist is the one who drew the logo. Yes, we have a logo... Why would she have to try so hard?

After admiring and rereading the invitation for The Academy Ball, I quickly rsvp'd and plan to call my best gay guy friend, Kenny, to coordinate outfits immediately. The one thing I love about Kenny is that we both shop at the same stores. The only time I can shop for Husband at J McLaughlin (JM) is completely against his will. I secretly buy the boys all matching outfits from JM, so Kenny is the perfect outfit planner. Before every vacation we always discuss outfits and, of course, before every big date Kenny has with his boyfriend, we plot.

Today I am going to the first Academy Ball Committee meeting. "Kenny, what are you doing?" I say after he answers hello in his usual singsong manner. He loves to pretend he is Anna Wintour's personal assistant. He is a personal assistant but not for anyone nearly that famous, but the Annenbergs probably have more money. He gets to drive their cars (Porsche) and stay in all of their estates in Palm Beach, Maine and Wyoming. Those are just the ones in The USA. Kenny could be my brother, but with blond hair and brown eyes. He is always in head-to-toe Burberry and Stubbs & Wooten velvet slippers with his initials. He carries an oversized Hermès Birkin bag as a brief case.

"Hello, Elizabeth, how can I help you?" Kenny jokes.

"What do I wear to my first Academy Ball committee meeting? I don't want to appear like I'm trying too hard," I sigh. Kenny's employers don't even have to sit on committees or go to events, they are so AT. Actually, he is so above all this MC behavior, he doesn't completely get it.

"What about that new Ann Taylor suit, pink tweed. You bought it when I was with you." Kenny is so good.

"Great idea, thanks." We kiss as we hang up.

I met with my personal trainer, Nicki, today. A lot of us use the same trainer. It's strange. We worked out really hard so my butt is sore, but I am happy.

I am wearing pink tweed sling backs and a matching suit. My long brown hair is appropriately blown out. Going to these meetings is a lot like going to our tea group. There's the ringleader, and then there are my friends. Everyone is pleasantly awkward, as usual. There are always co-chairs in charge of the committee. I guess they never chair things alone. The same person, Kitty Kimmel, always chairs the committees on which I participate. Kitty is an UB extraordinaire. Everyone else loves her, and she is gorgeous.

Back in high school, she was in love with and dated Duncan Wilson from Episcopal. Duncan went to Lake Forest College with us. Once, by accident, when I was really, really drunk on grain alcohol shots, I slept with him. Kitty found out at lacrosse practice and practically got me to leave college. She tried to make everyone hate me. We've since moved on and now are friends again. Sort of. Kitty is the one that asked me to be in the Tea Group. Her mother-in-law was in the original tea group. Now, she has asked me to be on the Academy Ball Committee, and also the Philadelphia Antique Show. I think it's one of those, "keep your friends close and your enemies closer," situations. The issue is I am still afraid of her as she has tons of money and an extremely prestigious last name.

The whole social season in Philadelphia revolves around the Art Museum, the Orchestra, and PAFA. It starts in September with opening night of the Orchestra and runs all the way through spring. You really don't even have the summer off because summer is when you meet with the committee.

Being co-chair is almost like being the most popular girl in school, but it is different somehow. With SCs, there is no more popularity, no one really cares if they are well liked or not. Eventually, popularity wears off and SS takes over. You can be the biggest jerk, but if your last name is Astor, all of a sudden you are the most popular person. I just had a chemical peel, and a couple of weeks ago, botox injections in my forehead, which I openly admit. SCs are the type of people who

43

lie about things. They have things done, and they won't admit to it. I am wearing my gold charm bracelet, a fabulous gold cocktail ring and pearl earrings.

I recently sent out invitations for my son's birthday party, which is to be held at the Camden Aquarium. I had perfect "fish" invitations sent out. They are actually rubber fish, better than any other invitation. Cute!

So walking down Broad Street, I'm feeling very confident. Of course, you show up on day one of the committee dreading all the responsibilities that you are going to have, but you prepare to purchase a page and pull your weight. At the end of the day, it's all about getting your picture in the paper and your name on that invitation. To elevate oneself to have extraordinary wealth, to be an "It" couple, but most of all, to become a Philadelphia Socialite—is a title we all want. You have to be on committees. "It" girls are always on the best committees. SC wanna-be socialites will sit on any committee they are asked to join. I don't even read an invitation when it comes. I immediately look on the back to see who's on the committee. Let's face it, we all know when each event is anyway, but what we really care about is whether any of our friends are on this committee. If yes, why wasn't I asked? An AT will find her name on the back of an invitation without even knowing she was on the committee. Now, *that's* success, because you did not even have to do anything. "It" is all about the name!

Just as I'm walking to the Committee Meeting, my cell phone rings. Cell phones are a funny thing. Everyone has one these days, and it's almost like a status thing. If you are on your cell phone, you're more popular; more wanted. The more people call you, the more important you are. It's like no one can be alone anymore. Quite frankly, I like the peace and quiet. Anyway, it's Colby. Colby is one of my best friends, so I *always* have to take her calls. Colby is freaking out because another one of her nannies quit.

As I walk into the room, I get the North South from Kitty. So, I get off of my cell phone, and I sit down around the table for the committee meeting. All of us have sparkling diamond rings and nice clothes. Of course, I am sizing up everyone's rings. Jewelry is a major distraction. Everyone has blond hair, except me. Everyone is just so awkward, so quiet! It is making me self-conscious. No one can be outgoing or be themselves.

Thank God, the meeting starts. Kitty gets up to welcome everyone and talks about upcoming events for the year. The standoffishness has ended because we start learning the details for the ball. "Thank you all for coming today," Kitty begins. As Kitty stands, I notice she is wearing beautiful silk ivory Tahari pants with a pattern and matching shoes. She has on a wrap blouse and looks very Kate Hepburn, who went to Baldwin and Bryn Mawr College. "This is going to be the most exciting Academy Ball ever, because this year, we have the best committee!" Kitty says enthusiastically. "I am so grateful to be the co-chair. Thank you for this honor. Kit and I have been coming to The Academy Ball our whole lives." She pauses, looking each of us in the eye before moving on. "I am the reason they created The Young Friends committee 10 years ago. I remember as a little girl watching my Grandmother dress for the Academy Ball and thinking it was the most extravagant, elegant affair. When I was old enough, I would attend with my Grandmother and loved every minute of it. The Mayor would always ask me to dance, and I would feel like a princess."

Blah, blah, blah. All Kitty does is talk about herself. *Aren't we going to hear how to raise money to save the oldest music hall in the country?* I am thinking to myself as we learn that Oscar de la Renta is to be our Guest of Honor that evening. This is more exciting than anything in the world. I mean, he is like God. Next to Lee Radziwill, I don't think there is a more famous person that I want to meet. I can picture it now, being on the committee, maybe I can get my picture taken with him. I can be in every paper and every magazine in Philadelphia. Better yet, I could be in the *New York Times* Style Section (The Bible) or *Town and Country.* That is the be-all, end-all. I have a religion. It is Oscar and NYT Style Section. *W* and *Vogue* never cover any parties in Philadelphia, but Oscar de la Renta commands international coverage. This is like a dream come true. I'm sure that he will find me super-charming and super-interesting. We'll have so much to talk about. I've been all over the world and even lived in Zimbabwe. He and I will get along famously and we will be laughing and chatting, and everyone will be snapping our picture. I won't wear Oscar so as to not be too obviously sucking up to him. I have it all planned out. So now at the meeting I am very excited and determined to work hard and get the recognition that I deserve.

All of this is running through my mind and I am clearly not paying attention or listening to a word Kitty is saying when she looks at me and says, "Okay, Elizabeth?"

I am trying to look into her eyes to appear that I care what she is saying, I must have seemed like I was volunteering for something, because the next thing I hear myself say is "yes." *What did I agree to?*

After the meeting ends I find Mimi. "Mimi please tell me what I agreed to," I say with my pleading eyes. "You are my best friend in the world so please don't tell anyone I was on another planet."

"The raffle committee. You agreed to head up the raffle committee," Mimi laughs. *Lovely.* Now I get to spend the next nine months slaving away to obtain free dinners and overnight stays at hotels. Just great!

On my way home, I wonder what it would be like to be Lee Radziwill. She is my goddess. It must have been incredible to be sisters with Jackie O. I mean, to know all the people that she knows, travel where she has, and also, to be so cute and petite and well dressed all at once. Plus, she married a prince. There aren't that many of them out there that are of appropriate age. I know he's only a Polish prince, but hey, he's a prince! I bet she is really good friends with Oscar de la Renta. "Say it Right," by Nelly Furtado plays on the radio.

Then my mother calls. Of course, she is calling about skiing--that is all my mother does. Some people go for several plastic surgeries, some people are alcoholics, and others love to cook. All I know is what my mother does, and she skis all the time. But, she also pulls me right back to reality. "Elizabeth, I am planning to take Greye to Vermont in January, is that okay with his school?" Mommie is not really asking.

"Yes, Mommie, I will let them know," I say thinking *this is next year.*

"What week shall I keep him?" Mommie asks.

"The week of Academy Ball is good because I will be frantic. It's always the last weekend in January," I say, as I flip through the radio stations.

"Okay, I will mark my calendar."

"All right, Mommie." Mommie makes kissing noises as she hangs up. We all ski. Husband and I ski, our sons' ski. Skiing is a very preppy thing to do, but Mommie skis too much. She insists on going practically every week during the season. While it's true in the Northeast we have lovely resorts only a few hours from us, Mommie skis at Stratton, which is over five hours away. I don't like the idea of my mother driving all that way every week by herself. But she is obsessed and says it makes her happy. I know it's important to have a passion. But every week? *Doesn't she get cold?*

Chapter VI

THE RULES

Mimi and I are on our way to Kitty's for an Academy Ball committee meeting. I am praying Kitty refrains from talking about herself the whole time. Mimi drives a typical Main Line car, a navy blue BMW convertible, with a khaki interior. Totally flashy for her otherwise preppy appearance. "Pippa's pissing off her new in-law family," Mimi says ever so casually.

"Really, how?" I ask.

"Well, she only buys gifts for the cousins and sister in-laws that she deems appropriate, while slighting her husband's sister." Mimi finds this amusing.

See, when you are new to a group, same as when you are new to an area, there are certain rules you have to adhere to. As long as your goal is to fit in, and we both know Pippa wants to excel. Not just fit in, win. It is kind of like wanting to be an actress or a star. You grow up looking at all the pictures of the society women. Not Paris Hilton-- think Amanda Hearst. They look so deliriously happy and effortlessly glamorous. Wanting to be a movie star is not a goal one normally has when growing up on the Main Line. I would die if I had camera people following me and people approaching me while I was dining at Washington Square. For the most part, I like my privacy. Socialites have SS and respect, it is so much more understated.

We are driving very slowly down the street checking out everyone's cars.

"I heard Pippa is doing a fund raiser for her step-children's school and put a picture of a trash can on the invite," Mimi adds.

"Why?" That sounds gross.

"It is a clean-up project, kinda thing," Mimi explains.

"Oh, Okay," I get it.

"In the trash can, however were cigarettes and beer cans. The school flipped!" Mimi laughs. OMG, that is terrible. When you are new, even if your in-laws have all the right connections, club memberships, and your "children" go to the right school, you still have to prove yourself. Pippa is automatically receiving and sending Christmas cards to the right list. Now she just has to play by the other rules to get truly accepted.

We enter Kitty's house and the meeting has begun, so we sit down quietly while a staff member hands us our agenda. I can't help but notice Kitty's coat closet is slightly ajar; she has only quilted hangers for hanging her lovely coats. *Note to self: redo coat closet with plush hangers.* I get distracted by the strangest things.

"We are going to be using Robertson's florist for the table decorations." Kitty is discussing the ball décor.

"Isn't that expensive?" another committee woman asks.

"Kit and I will be donating the décor," Kitty certainly put an end to that conversation. However generous, I know secretly Kitty would never allow an event with her name on it to have carnations, or, god forbid, balloons; so, true to form, this kind donation is not kind but rather selfish. The Academy would be better off if she simply donated the money she is spending on the flowers.

After the meeting, we have light refreshments and I walk into the kitchen where Mimi and Kitty are laughing. "Yes, I have Kit running all of my errands today; I mean he owns three companies, but he is running to CVS for my tampons!" Kitty exclaims, so proud of herself. *Gross!* Too much information.

Mimi and I leave shortly after that. "I guess I'm going to have to call Nimi's about the gift bags," Mimi says. That's Neiman-Marcus.

"Oh, that would be such a nice gift bag. I hope they'll do it." Knowing they will, as Mimi is their top client. Not just her, but her fiancé and entire family. Mimi's fiancé loves to buy her clothes. I would never dream of letting Husband buy me clothes.

"I'll call you later," I say, thanking Mimi for dropping me at my car, which I had left at the restaurant where Allegra and I are meeting for lunch. "You sure you don't want to come?" I ask.

"No, can't. Have to meet Pippa about some other committee." Mimi looks annoyed, but I know she is not. "Wouldn't it be good," by Nik Kershaw blares from her radio as she pulls away.

Allegra always makes several reservations (not in her name, of course, not wanting to be hated for last-minute cancellations or no-shows). As

I wait for her, I think more about poor Pippa's situation. She's a great person. I know she has absolutely not turned down a single invitation for parties or committees since marrying her Pew husband. Pippa knows socially acceptable behavior and rules. Plus, I know she is reciprocating, having everyone for cocktails, cookouts and always writing thank you notes. At least, I hope she's writing thank you notes. *Oh god*, I have not sent one to Kitty yet for tea. Note to self.

In walks Allegra in a blue and red silk printed scarf from Hermès she is wearing as a top with cute navy capris and super-high red heels. She looks so tan! "Hello," we air kiss.

"Spot anything good we can take?" Asks Allegra right away. We have this habit of steeling potpourri, napkins and silver from our favorite restaurants. I, for one, take the printed napkins in the bathroom to use in my own home. It shows I dine at the best spots. Then when friends are over, they are like, "Oh, I love The Fountain Room at The Four Seasons!" Also, I like leaving with a nice wine glass. Husband gets so embarrassed, rightfully so, but Allegra got me hooked.

"Not yet, but I wasn't looking," I add, noticing Allegra is wearing a Hidalgo ring. Just like the one I bought myself after having Field. "Nice ring, Allegra" I say, staring at her, like "I know you copied me." Jewelry is my biggest distraction.

"Oh, yeah, I've got like three others. They are my new favorite." She smiles, looking at her menu. *Since When!?* "So, how were your first few committee meetings? Was that SC there?" Allegra purrs in her Greek accent.

"Who, Kitty?" I ask not wanting a response. "Of course, she is the fucking co-chair. She went on and on about herself as usual and, of course, I got stuck with the worst possible job," I whine. I hate myself when I complain.

"Elizabeth, I don't even know why you do all these committees. Kitty just makes your life miserable. She is not a good friend to you." Allegra says all of this matter-of- factly. Allegra sticks up for me but also thinks I'm asking for misery by spending time in Kitty's company. I can't help it; I like her for some odd reason. She's pretty.

"I know, but I have to give back. Otherwise, what else would I do?" Allegra is right. After all, she knows the whole back-story with Duncan. She stood by my side through it all. Kitty may be well loved on the Main Line, because of her in laws money. But, at least I have Allegra, Colby, Mimi and Pippa. "Plus, her hair looked so long and luscious, I could not help myself," I say. "I went right up to her, and as I was complimenting her hair, I touched it and could feel the extensions," I add like a true private investigator. "She had the audacity to say to me she has been taking really good care of it, taking a new multi-vitamin and not highlighting as much. Can you believe her?" I exclaim.

At home that evening I pull a piece of my stationary out. It is an ivory card, very thick stock. With my name in gold script at the top and right below it, centered, is a little ship's wheel; after all I do live at the shore. (Even if I am in denial.) I want to be polite but not a kiss ass. I write:

"Dear Kitty," I then stop.

My mind wanders. I will think of a way to politely find out if Pippa is writing her notes. Or maybe they just don't like her because they think she is loud. You can't get drunk or say obnoxious things about people to strangers when you are trying to fit it. Oh God, I remember my friend Topher, from The Haverford School, married that atrocious girl from Nebraska. It was sad, really. I heard mental disease runs in her family, but she would get so drunk at our parties. She is literally never invited to anything unless the co- chair is desperate! Colby could have cared less if she was drunk, she had just never met anyone who hadn't heard of *Town & Country*. I know Pippa is working really hard on her committees, obtaining corporate sponsors, but it just may not be enough. Note to self: *call Pippa for cocktails*. Pippa wore Essie "sugar daddy" the entire time during her first two years at her law firm, willing herself to meet one. She did.

I continue to write:

"Dear Kitty,

Thank you so much for having me to your lovely tea.

Your home is as beautiful, as are you!

xoxo,

Yours,

Elizabeth."

Short and sweet.

Chapter VII

ALL ABOUT ME--A TRUE SC

I am neither thin nor fat. I am a size 8. I am 5'4" and have normal proportions. If I had to pin-point it, I hate my hips. My best feature is my face. I glow and have light freckles—a true Scot. I have brown hair and blue eyes, which is the best contrast. Husband told me I had the prettiest eyes he had ever seen, and he would know because he is an eye surgeon. I fell for that. I am fairly outgoing and articulate. I'm the type of person who always wants the world to be a prettier, nicer place to live. One where everyone speaks proper English, where lawns are properly manicured; a world where one dresses nicely and is polite and thoughtful. I had a friend in high school that always ended her sentences with the word "at." I would explain to her that you should not use a preposition at the end of a sentence. So, she would says things like, "So where is it at, Bitch!" Just to provoke me.

I think that I get my proper English obsession from my mother. I remember when I was in the ninth grade, Mommie went to a school Open House. In English class she raised her hand and asked, "What can be done about teaching children proper English and stop using the word "like"?" For some reason, my teacher was so shocked by this question that the next day she decided to repeat the story in class. Of course, she knew it was my mother at Open House. Parents always sit in the same seat their child does. I was embarrassed, especially because my teacher made such a big deal about it. Now, I must admit, I agree with my mother. I hate agreeing with her. I like it much better when my son says yes, instead of yeah, and says thank you and please.

I just hate it when I am in Philadelphia, a beautiful historic city, and I see "yucky" everywhere. I like the world to be fresh, clean, light, neat and lovely. I mean, I buy Yves St. Laurent mascara in its beautiful gold casing because it smells good. I don't even wear make-up, except to a party. Even then, I have someone else from Pierre and Carlo do it. I don't know how to put on anything but lipstick.

I read an article once that said women should spend less time being consumed about how they look. The woman who wrote "The Vagina Monologues" is doing a play about women and how much time they spend thinking about themselves/how they look and how women could be so much better as a cultural group if they spent less time thinking about their appearance. I must go see her play to learn what she has to say about all this, because I can't think of anything better than to think about myself and ways of improving my looks. Sometimes it scares me. After all, I went to college and have a degree in Anthropology. So I am smart, right? But I seem to spend a great deal of time and mental anguish thinking about what to wear. Truly!

I grew up doing all kinds of fun things in the summer. Besides camp at Taqua in Chesapeake, Maryland, where we went sailing and water skiing, I've lived in Martha's Vineyard and in Maine for two summers, once in Bar Harbor, once in Prout's Neck. Both were very preppy. I also lived at Lake Winnipesaukee in New Hampshire one summer. Mommie and I went skiing in Argentina and New Zealand. I also traveled Europe for two summers.

I should also explain why I have some perspective on SCs. I learned a few things. Although I grew up on the Main Line, Radnor to be specific, my family actually comes from a middle-class background. Daddy grew up in a steel mill town in West Virginia. While my family is definitely very smart, well read, well traveled and of comfortable means, I was never rich and my parents made it a point to be sure I had a dose of reality and perspective on the world. So while I grew up surrounded by the wealthy and the wanna be wealthiest, I came from a more modest background. This is why I understand the difference between an SC and an AT. I guess it was growing up around all of that wealth that bred me into an SC, but now I know better. I learned the hard way. I used to want to be like them.

Not only did I grow up in a nice town, but I also had the good fortune of going to college in a nicer town, Lake Forest, Illinois, home of Lake Forest College. This is where I was born; so not only did I live in Radnor but I also get to tell people I was born in Lake Forest (two "right" addresses that are very impressive to an SC). I went to college with people from families like Pillsbury, Jack Daniels, with daughters of Generals in the Army, and daughters whose parents owned football teams. You name it. Plus, Lake Forest is crawling with lots of young married mommies that are social climbing all over the place in Chicago. Illinois is ostentatious, many cars have vanity plates—especially Lake Forest. So I was treated to a double entrée of growing up in a town with SCs and going to college in a town with SCs. If you look in *The Official Preppy Handbook*, all the towns mentioned were represented at Lake Forest College. In fact, Lake Forest itself was in *The Official Preppy Handbook*, both the college and the town. I think preppies were the original SCs. It was great preparation.

Having someone talk behind your back is one of the biggest fears of SCs. That's why it is so important to wear the right uniform (jewelry, shoes, and clothes) and drive the right car. "It" girls always have the coolest cars. I drive a white Jaguar, but don't get too excited. I call it the econo Jag; it's the X class. It's not as nice as the larger ones, but it is still a beautiful white car with camel interior. It matches my wardrobe. I love British cars and always coveted a Jaguar. When I was growing up, no one drove Bentleys. But the Jag was the ultimate fancy car, so I had to have one. We all have oriental rugs as our floor mats and pot pourri in the ashtray. Even though we all smoke we wouldn't dream of ashing in the ashtray. That should have been in *The Official Preppy Handbook*. I think having "older person" or "mature" items at a young age is very elegant, classy and humorous all at the same time. I worship C.Z. Guest. That is why I consigned all of my wool coats and only wear furs, drive a Jag and wear lots and lots of jewelry. In fact, I get a lot of my fashion inspiration from women in there 60s and 70s. Before my Jag, I drove a station wagon, when I was, 25. It was so cute with beautiful leather interior. I must admit I ended up trading that in because it made me feel too suburban housewife, even though I do admire other people in them. I don't want to be total cliché with the two children, dog and station wagon.

One would never know that I once worked. I was a publicist for a boutique firm after I graduated from college. I saw a lot there! People hired us to make them stars. Out of town bankers relocate to Philadelphia. They are clueless about what boards to be on. Our firm took care of those introductions. There's a lot more to being a publicist than placing stories in the newspaper. You have no idea. I have a theory that being a working mother is coming back into style. A lot of "It" girls have jobs now. I completely look up to Aerin Lauder. Enough about me, back to SCs!

Cool Social Climbers:

The Miller Sisters

Marina Rust

Lauren Dupont

Shafi Roepers

Amanda Brooks

Rene Rockefeller

Dawn Steel

Samantha Boardman

Grace Kelly

Babe Paley (I love anyone who smokes)

Caroline Bissett Kennedy

Tinsley Mortimer

Suzy Welch

Shoshanna Lonstein

Diana Vreeland

Jacqueline Onassis

Monica Lowinsky

Jessica Seinfeld

Slim Keith

Queen Noor

Plum Sykes

Ricky Lauren

Eliza Reed Bolen (too many names. Just say Oscar)

Kate Spade

Vanessa Getty

Nan Kempner

Betsy Bloomingdale

Celerie Kemble

Pamela Churchill Harriman

Truman Capote

Chapter VIII

The Salon

Inside Pierre and Carlo, or more importantly, inside The Bellevue Hotel, I contemplate life. Pierre and Carlo is located at The Bellevue, the premier hotel in Philadelphia, the one where I made my debut and where all the highbrow events are held. It's almost as old as The Academy of Music, which is right next door. It has the most elegant entranceway—you feel like a princess every time you walk in.

I could not decide what to wear this weekend to a cocktail party Husband and I have to attend at the shore. My favorite part of being at a salon is when they wash your hair or put you under the dryer. Then no one can talk to you and I can visualize my closet. I have the cutest brown silk top and pencil skirt, from Barami. The skirt has feathers adorning the bottom and I look fabulous in chocolate. How brilliant, I will wear that! See the hair salon is really helpful. I can be so focused here.

"Hi, honey," Pippa smiles as she walks over to the seat next to me to be washed.

"Hello, Miss Pippa. How did you escape work today to be here?" I ponder. Pippa has the bombshell blond thing going on. She is only like, 5'5", but she has strong athletic legs, large breasts and a tiny, tiny waist. Blond hair so blond you can't believe. Note to self: *ask Peter what they do to make her hair that blond!*

"I need a touch-up. Plus, no one ever asks where I am." Pippa leans back to be washed. With a Pew as a husband, it's no wonder people don't ask questions.

Later, back at our seats, our stylist assistants' bring us chai teas. Chai tea is supposed to be better for you than coffee, something about it being from India where they are so much more in tune with life. I would love to be a Buddha for a month and get all New Age and really find myself. Note to self: *find guru.* I think it would help me be a better person. Honestly, I doubt I could handle the sleeping arrangements at an Ashram. But the best I can do is spend the day in glorious Philadelphia. They serve champagne, of course, at Pierre and Carlo, but we would not be caught dead drinking during the day, at least not in public. I love living at the shore away from "it all," but this is where I truly feel comfortable.

Growing up here makes knowing the rules so inbred. If I were from out of town, I would be a total SC too. Philadelphia is just so subtle. You can't try too hard, or you are considered tacky. No one would dream of hiring a publicist unless it were for charity. Socialites are devoted philanthropists. Philadelphia being one of the oldest cities, and here in The Bellevue, one of the oldest buildings, everyone is practically off the boat. The Mayflower folks don't wear too much of anything, make-up, jewelry, furs or high fashion. Even if a Muffy lives in a huge estate in Paoli, she drives herself around in her Range Rover. All coming from European descent gives us a sense of stature.

"Did you hear about the new fund raiser for children?" Asks "no ones hair is that blond" while looking over an invitation.

"No, who are the co-chairs?" I ask, very interested.

"Oh, typical SCs like M Night Shyamalan and Pearlman's new wife." Pippa glances at me.

"Who?" I ask. All "It" Philadelphians that make it big get forced into giving back, at least with their name.

"I can't remember her name. You know, that girl you went to school with who became a newscaster in New York City. Then she married a Pearlman, so now she's back." Pippa looks up at the ceiling trying to remember her name.

"You mean the Clothier girl? I heard Larry Kane got her that job. Anyone can be a newscaster," I say with envy.

"Yes, she's totally NR and bff with The Cohns, Roberts and Lenfests, and they are all heading up this children's charity. Want to go?" Pippa knows all about NR. I love Pippa. We are old friends, but her not ethnically desired family is by no stretch AT. Rumor has it, although she has never admitted it, her father is Jewish. The thing is, Pippa went to the right schools and learned how to act like a WASP, and so she is terrific despite it.

"Sure, why not," I say, sipping my tea and opening *W.* I know for a fact Pippa does not really know any of those people, but now that she is a Pew she acts like they are her best friends. *Typical!*

"Elizabeth, I almost totally forgot, I still have Field's present," Pippa says.

"Oh, you are sweet," I say, turning the page. It sounds like she is fitting in better than Mimi portrayed. I really do love her; she is an old, trusted friend.

Chapter IX

CATTY WOMEN

As I walk up to the Union League bar I cannot help but notice a beautiful portrait of a pale, familiar woman. *No, it can't be.* I approach the painting. Yes, it is none other than Kitty Kimmell, in profile. I grab Colby's arm and drag her to the portrait. "Look," I say, as I stare at the wall.

"Why is she looking to the side?" Colby looks dumbfounded.

"Who cares?" I say, grabbing champagne off of a butlered tray. As we walk through the Union League admiring Nelson Shank's private collection I am so jealous that Kitty's picture hangs on the same walls as Princess Di and The Pope. This is so typical. Her in laws are probably best friends with Nelson. And then there she is! *Fuck!*

"Hi, Ladies," Kitty smiles.

"Kitty! I just saw your drop-dead picture." I try to keep a brave face.

"Oh, my god, I am so embarrassed." *Right.* "I mean, I never would commission a painter," Kitty says, gloating. *Commission? Who says that?*

"Nelson begged me to pose for him, he said no make-up, no hair styling, no jewelry. I was, like, what else do I have?" She is sooooooo proud of herself. Colby's face is fuscia. *Shit*, she "commissioned" Nelson to do the girls. Kitty's such a UB.

Instead, "Did he pick out the dress?" I ask.

"Yes," Kitty smiles as I realize she is wearing it—*Loser*. It's a silk Nina Ricci dress. The dress is sophisticated.

"Is that the one?" I say, pointing to her outfit. I will not let her get away with this.

"Yes," her pale skin actually flushes.

I am actually getting sick to my stomach! "I love it," I say, turning to Colby. "Honey, let's get a drink." I drag her back to the bar once more to get another look at the painting. "It was painted five years ago." I look at Colby in horror.

"I can't believe she still has the dress," Colby adds.

Down in the smoking room of The Union League Colby and I take a break. Her feet are hurting. The smoking room is the only room you are allowed to smoke in at The Union League. It is very well decorated, comfortable and has a special expensive ventilation system so it doesn't smell. Colby is humiliated she is paying (a lot) for something Kitty got for free. "Did Nelson really want to paint Kitty that badly?" Colby sulks.

"Honey, you know the Kimmels probably have ... portraits painted and paid for them," I try to comfort C... have made that up you know," I add.

"It's going to be over 100 grand for this painting," Colby and I both notice Kit walk by with a friend.

"They are never together, or even in the same room," Colby observes.

Neither are you and your husband, "Kitty's too busy being an SC."

On the way home in the car "Heart and Soul," by Huey Lewis and the news blares on the radio.

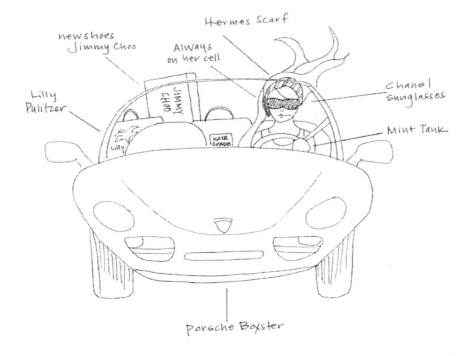

newshoes
Jimmy Choo

Hermes Scarf

Always
on her cell

Lilly
Pulitzer

Chanel
sunglasses

Mint Tank

Porsche Boxster

Chapter X

FAMILY

"It" girls come from the right family. Mommie, is an interesting breed of eccentric. You can't even call her a social climber. She is from a different era. And she is not from the Main Line, another blip in my SS. Mommie did the Cinderella Ball for her debut. We *all* call her "Mommie." When I was little I tried to call her Mom like everyone else called his or her mother and she quickly corrected me. "I am not your mom; I am either your mother or your mommie." So I went with "Mommie." It is easier to rhyme with. She smokes with a cigarette filter, which is about three inches long. It is sort of like Cruella de Vil's. She says things like, "Wine should be served at castle temperature." As if most people have been to a castle and know the temperature. She ate at The White House once, but that's NO castle. (Sometimes I try to use slang. I think it makes me seem down to earth.) She also says things like, "Never do anything to harm or scar your face. People always like you because you are pretty." Also, you can never chew gum in front of my mother; it is her biggest pet peeve. She thinks it is so unlady-like.

But did I mention her Hermès Kelly bag is never devoid of a pack of Trident, cinnamon flavor. I picture her driving in her Lincoln Town car alone blowing bubbles and cracking her gum.

I remember when my first son was born, and he was developing cognitively. She called me in a panic and said that we had to discuss the fact that my son is brilliant. Although I do think that my son is brilliant; sometimes he can ramble on and on about various aspects of fish right down to species as well as all kinds of trains to the point where I don't even understand him. I quickly reminded Mommie that all parents and grandparents think that their children are brilliant (even though he really is). Someone in this family has to be level-headed. Mommie responded without a beat, "I never thought you were brilliant." *Lovely!*

Mommie, like Colby, has never married her true love--yet. Of all three of her husbands, not one of them has been her true love. Like a true SC, my mother always married for things like money and security (or unplanned pregnancy). Daddy, second of her three husbands, wasn't exactly rich, but he definitely was secure, which provided me with such a great father. Also, I call him Daddy. Even though my mother was a Mommie, my father never really gave me a preference, but since I was calling her Mommie, I called him Daddy. My grandmother was married four times. It seems to run in the family. I wonder if I am going to have more than one husband? My Husband has always admitted that if I hadn't married him that I would have probably married much better. Being a doctor is good, but it is better if you're a developer, or have family money.

Daddy, the one with the beautiful, stately name, is very down to earth and stable. His father was the Vice President of a steel company, but he still wasn't rich, which is why I am still social climbing. Daddy was the complete opposite of Mommie when I was growing up. He always said to me, "Don't act like a princess," and, "You are smart--You can be whatever you want to be when you grow up." Don't get me wrong. It is not like I ever yearned for anything. I have always lived in a beautiful house, went to a really nice college, had beautiful clothes, traveled all over Europe, Africa and Asia, and get jewelry for every occasion possible. I went to etiquette school, white glove dancing class and learned French. Basically, I could never ask for anything, but the whole point of social climbing is to be better than that, to be an "It" Girl. (BTW I hate the term "It" Girl. It is so 2001--but no one has come up with anything better.)

The main difference between my parents is that Daddy is always being supportive and Mommie is always being suggestive. For example, *maybe* I should lose five pounds or *maybe* I should do this with my sons or *maybe* I should do that for Husband. I am totally Daddy's Little Girl (DLG).

Daddy remarried, but unlike my mother, this is his final marriage. Daddy married someone way younger. Of course, they all do, right? Why else would god invent Botox? We have to stay young. She isn't a typical step-monster with a shoe closet the size of Kitty's. She is cool and nice to me, plus, since she is my age, we shop together and do the whole spa thing.

Chapter XI

THE HOME

When I get home that evening, my two yummy little boys are there waiting for me with their nana. Nana is what they call our nanny. Of course, what I really want to do is relax and watch TV. Children can be very draining with all of their questions and irrational demands. Field also has a habit of crying for anything Greye is playing with. Greye has a habit of crying every time Field is playing with on of his toys. My theory is that's why wine was invented. I am most excited to catch up on Entertainment Tonight and Access Hollywood. It is very important to find out what the stars are doing and wearing. I always like to hear what is going on in their lives, especially when it is bad. Somehow, it makes me feel better. *Is that horrible?*

Then Husband gets home—he is so cute. Not Vince Vaughn cute, but sooo cute. He is such an amazing father and a nice husband. He is also very smart. I had no idea he was this smart when I married him. I knew he was intelligent. He has a doctorate after all. But, he is brilliant. I mean, he is out fixing people's eyes all day. Who knew he would be so astute to become an Ophthalmologist as opposed to one of those other doctors who cut people open and work in the middle of the night? Ophthalmologists barely work and make all kinds of money. Husband's has a friend who is also an Ophthalmologist and he sets his schedule so he can sleep in till 9:00. Really. I'm so lucky I married somebody so sharp. His family does like Nascar and RVs', while wearing their finest linen suits. I was a bit of a shock to their system. Sophisticated people that live at the shore call people from the Main Line, shoebees. I don't even know what that term means. But Husband and I are well matched. I am completely devoted to Husband.

"How was your day, honey?" asks Husband.

I tell him about my first committee meeting, and how I was tricked into the raffle committee by a UB. "So now I am endlessly trying to obtain raffles. It has meant a lot of organizing."

Husband does not care to hear my problems. Mainly because I don't think he thinks I have problems. *But I really do!*

"What's for dinner?" Husband chides. He knows I don't cook.

"Ask Nana," I reply, giving him a dirty look, while opening a bottle of wine. Nana is my wife. At least that is what I call her. She does everything for me. I am not overly domestic in the slightest. In fact, I don't have a domestic bone in my body. But I want the house to look and smell nice. Nana runs all my errands: dry cleaner, grocery store, bank, *et al.* She also cleans the house, does all the laundry and makes the boys' dinner, not a very good dinner, but at least I don't have to do it. Nana and I definitely fight and get on each other's nerves, but I would be lost without her. She even makes my bed. One time she went to South America to visit her family and brought home truly atrocious gifts for the boys and us. The worst part was one of the gifts was a house decoration, so I had to display it. Yuck! I purposely put it in a spot where the baby would ruin it.

I have to say that I love my house! I know that Margate isn't exactly Locust Valley, New York or Chappaqua, but I just love my house. And since I must live down here because of my husband's amazing job, when I'm home watching Entertainment Tonight and catching up on all the stars, I'm so happy.

I painted my living room the perfect red. There are pheasants everywhere. I love leopard print. I have accents all over the house. My umbrella is even leopard, not real just printed. I think the reason I like to decorate so much with animals is it reminds me of all the safaris I went on--ten to be exact. I have been on safari on foot, horseback, boat, Land Rover, bus, you name it. Animals are immensely cute. I just love them, especially my adorable Chesapeake Bay retriever (way cooler than having just a regular lab), Penny. My dining room has wainscoting and my kitchen is the perfect neutral beige, full of pineapples and roosters, and has the perfect view of the water. My bedroom is yellow with monkeys all over it and my son's nursery has elephants and a safari mural painted on the walls, and my other son's has little sailboats. When we are on our boat on the water, we can look up at it because it sits up high; it is the cutest house on the hill.

All the other houses in our neighborhood are log cabins, where our house has a hunting/fishing lodge kind of feel. In the living room, the stonewall surrounding the fireplace is 18 feet tall. It is absolutely fabulous! There is nothing like being at home to get away from all those SCs who can make me feel inadequate.

Yellow is my favorite color in the whole world. You know how I like everything to be pretty? Well, yellow is just about the prettiest color; yellow tulips, yellow walls. I even wear a citrine on my right hand, a big eight-carat citrine. It looks nice next to my four-carat emerald cut diamond on my left hand. Eventually it will be a five+ canary diamond but that will be for our Ten-year anniversary. I love yellow! I try to dress in it all the time or as much as possible. The only thing I don't do is drive in it or swim in it. My pool is painted a very deep dark blue, and I have matching rafts, noodles and beach balls floating all over.

Allegra calls that night, fresh back from her trip to Hawaii. We are totally catching up about what everyone is doing and wearing. Allegra is learning to surf. "How is Academy Ball going?" Allegra asks.

"Okay, just a lot to organize in the beginning. Trying to figure out new cool raffles to get, that are better than last year's. Do you think Vespas' are cool?" I wonder.

"I would bid on a Mercedes," Allegra says. *Hmmm, I wonder how hard those are to get?*

"So tell me what else happened in Hawaii?" I ask. Allegra thinks all these committees are bullshit.

"I met someone," Allegra purrs. She sounds happy.

"What! Why isn't that the first thing you told me," I shout. I hope this is the one.

"Well I don't know. He is from Philadelphia weirdly enough." That's convenient.

"Why was he there? What's his name?" I am beyond excited.

"Frank, same surfing camp as me." Lots of single people do those types of trips, I hear.

"Did you kiss him?" I am so junior varsity. It's just like college.

"Elizabeth you're a dork!" Allegra is as excited as I am.

"What are you doing tomorrow?" Allegra asks, changing the subject because she does not want to jinx it.

Allegra is very secure with her SS. Allegra has light brown hair, with perfect highlights and deep dark brown eyes. Her skin is olive with a shimmer. She is meant to be in a bikini. She has perfect legs, and a great chest, which she always shows off. I think I noticed Colby's husband checking it out. Allegra is also 5'4" but with a perfectly flat stomach.

"Nails," I throw out there hoping she can come. We plan to meet the next day at Blooming Nails. Blooming Nails is one of those Korean nail salons, but it is not dirty or gross. It's not nearly as expensive as going to Pierre and Carlo where I usually get my manis and pedis. When I absolutely need one and can't get an appointment or know I won't be in the city, I go to Blooming Nails. It is fabulous. They put hot towels on your neck while you get your pedi and then while you are drying, a masseuse comes around and rubs your neck and your arms with hot towels. Nothing can be better for $40. Plus, at Pierre and Carlo, everyone listens to your conversation and repeats it.

SOCIAL CLIMBERS SAYINGS:

Cute!

Darling

Charming

BFF (best friends forever)

That's just not done

Authentic

Affluent

Fabo

That's really looked down upon

Love your body

Can you believe she did/said that?

That's Tops!

N.O.C.D (Not our class dear)

"It" Couple (which is so 2001)

Swanky

Subtle

Overstated

Outdone

Horrible

Dull

Detest

Impeccable Lineage

Proper

Pretentious

Perfect, Powerful and Polished!

Icky

Messy

Jet–setter

Disgusting

Keeping up appearances

Impressed

All I care about…

Envy

That's very cosmopolitan

Smashing

Ciao (over-use of foreign sayings is annoying)

Cool

You know you love me

Awesome

Phony

TTFN (ta ta for now)

Status

Breeding

Toodles

Swell

Brilliant

Nifty

Cellie, Mani, Pedi, Lunchie (putting an "ie" on the end of words makes it sound cuter but is also trés irritating)

I have nothing to wear

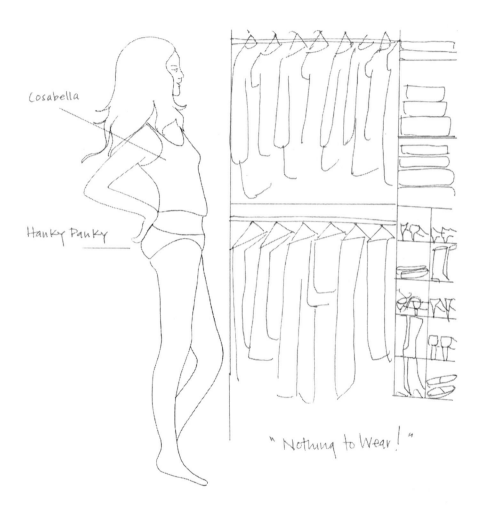

Cosabella

Hanky Panky

" Nothing to Wear ! "

I am sooooooo busy

Love You

Honey

Wannabe

Sweetie

Double Deal (second marriage)

That is so bourgeois

I'm allergic to polyester (not possible; it's synthetic)

Affected (Aunt vs. Ant)

Refer to mansions as: the cottage, the lodge, and the cabin

BTW (by the way)

Shocking

Peace, Love and Gucci

Yucky

Tacky

That cost me more than you are worth/will make in a lifetime

EW!

Chapter XII

Friends

"It" girls have the right friends. Allegra lives in Devon, PA, and is originally from Rye, New York, another perfect SC town. Anyway, Allegra is titled aristocracy from Greece. So she is, by no stretch of the imagination, an SC. Allegra and I used to drink everything out of wine glasses in college, even our tomato juice for breakfast. We were roommates and best friends from the very start. We both love triple-strand pearls, Joan & David shoes, and Cartier roll rings. We were matched up because we both put on our college application that we could never live with anyone who chewed with his or her mouth open. Can you believe two people wrote the exact same inane request? We were *meant* to be best friends forever. Lake Forest College figured rather than trying to survey the whole freshman student body about chewing food, they would put us obviously high maintenance ladies in the same room. It worked. It could have backfired, we could have hated one another, but it was love at first air kiss.

Colby is married to a doctor (of course), but she says she married her third love (as opposed to her first love). I guess we can all say that in some way. He is not a useful doctor. He is only a general practitioner, so we can't get free advice from him. I was her maid of honor. Colby hates her husband now; I have lots of friends who hate their husbands. He does not respect her. Plus, he is always checking out other women or himself. His ego is monstrous. She says she daydreams of poisoning him. Colby and I call it the Cinderella syndrome--once you have him, you don't want him. When you are single, you daydream "The White Dream"—to be a bride. Once you are married, you daydream "The Black Dream"--the funeral. Growing up, Colby had a horse named Poppy. "It" girls have horses, or at least pretend to. Colby lives in Wayne in a huge, sprawling mansion. Her father is a well-known dermatologist.

My single friends give me lots of ammunition and stories that I can share with Husband, which makes him feel cool and hip and part of the scene. Husband can bribe his friends with the stories. For example, he'll call his friends and say, "If you want to know about the lesbian story then you better call me back." Or, "You better let me use your house in Deer Valley, or I won't tell you about the breast job story."

Pippa got breast implants, and we were all up one night at my house touching them. Part of the allure is that it makes Husband and his friends think that there is something sexual going on. Another example is when we went down to Miami for our birthdays and stayed at the Delano in South Beach. Mimi and Pippa decided to be lesbians for the weekend. None of us really minded. We act as if we're not judgmental. It was just kind of inconvenient because they were also being belligerently drunk at the same time. Husband loves to tell these types of stories to his friends. As a matter of fact, Husband's friends think that I have the most interesting friends and the most interesting stories that they have ever heard. I guess that's just because they are nerdy doctors and scientists. To them, boob jobs and lesbian encounters are interesting. For me, it is all just a part of my life. So that is why it is important to have both married and single friends.

It doesn't matter that Allegra isn't married, because she is titled aristocracy, and she comes from a super wealthy Greek family. She has homes in places like Monte Carlo, Santorini, and Portofino, and went to camp in Switzerland. She definitely gives me lots of good information. For example, she went water skiing with Princess Stephanie and knew about her boyfriend, the instructor, way before the tabloids. She loves to travel. It's sort of her signature trait. She's always traveling to places like Saint Jean Cap Ferrat, in the French Riviera, Basel, Saint Barts and Brazil. Allegra is a jewelry saleswoman for an international jeweler, which just happens to have their main office in Philadelphia. Which, is how she ended up here. And I am so unbelievably grateful to have her. She started her career at Sotheby's, the job that all girls get out of college where you make 12 grand a year, but you rub elbows with a lot of SCs and ATs. Her grandmother is best friends with the woman who owns Bvlgari. So obviously, Allegra has the best jewelry in the whole world. Allegra says I'm just like her grandmother, and I take that as a huge compliment, because, as I said, she is titled aristocracy. Allegra is my skinniest friend. She works out all the time, but it's because she isn't married with children. Once you have all that going on, you don't have as much time to stay in shape. Allegra is the type who wears fur coats and tons of jewelry to an EAGLES game. Colby and Allegra keep me updated on all the trends.

I shouldn't minimize my friendship with Colby. I mean, she equally has just as pertinent information as Allegra, even though she is not an heiress or an aristocrat. Colby always says she married her third love, but that it does not matter, as he is going to be more trustworthy and faithful. If she had married her first love (a drunk womanizer), she might be having good sex, but he wouldn't be nearly as nice to her. I think she is rethinking that theory now. Colby's husband is developing an evil temper. Now that they have children, he screams at them. Colby knows lots of interesting things. Colby worked for many years in fashion in New York City for people like Donna Karan and Isaac Mizrahi. Since her father is a dermatologist, she has access to all kinds of interesting medical information, such as what are the best injections and skin creams.

Colby and I both got Saabs when we graduated from college. Colby's was black and mine was "citron beige," a.k.a., gold. It matched my jewelry. I like being a little gaudy. Colby isn't as thin, but she is my best-dressed friend. Her clothes are all designer. Colby has three daughters who are enrolled at The West Hill School. Colby is a total DLG.

Pippa Pew married into a very well-known family in Philadelphia. She got married last summer in Sun Valley, Idaho. Naturally, Allegra's grandmother thought it was ridiculous that anyone would get married in August! It is too hot, August is for vacationing only. The wedding was a who's who of the United States. Naturally, she has the pent house at "10", the most prestigious building on Rittenhouse Square. They also have a house in Bryn Mawr. I must say, she is the biggest NR. Pippa is not even that smart, but she insisted on going to Law School. We all knew her motivation, or rather her law degree in "Mrs." She planned to join a prestigious firm and go after a senior partner. Well, it worked! She worked for two years as a junior partner and ended up with a Pew. Sadly, when they met, he was married with two children, but I guess her breast implants came in handy because he left his wife for Pippa. Everyone was very drunk at her wedding, including her mother who is supposedly a reformed drinker. It was very funny. Husband and I were by far the poorest people in the room. We are always up for a good vacation, and when it is a friend's wedding, we always try to combine the two. Pippa is always thin. Again, she does not have children yet. She now claims to have two, the stepchildren. She loves to talk about how hard it is to be a mother. *As if*! But the Pew name has not secured Pippa's place in society. Don't get me wrong, she's in with a lot of important people. The First Wives Club, however, just isn't interested in a home wrecker. Kitty claims she is friends with the ex wife, which is why she hates Pippa. The real reason is The Kimmel family isn't as rich as The Pew's. The Pew's own oil.

Mimi Montgomery is my craziest, most fun, party girl friend. Every time Mimi gets a new apartment her mother re-does her slipcovers to match the walls. She prefers Pierre Frey. Mimi just bought a house in Berwyn. She is always up for a good time, and is engaged to be married next summer. Her wedding will be at The Equinox in Manchester, Vermont. We are all in the wedding. I think she is having 12 brides' maids. Mimi is more like me, an average weight. She is extraordinarily plain looking, but in the right way. She has bright green eyes, a pretty smile, freckled face and dark blond hair with not a lot of highlights, always in a layerless bob. We've all been friends since we were little, except Allegra. Allegra met them slowly as they visited me at Lake Forest College. Allegra came to see me on The Main Line during summer break. We were all ski-lift operators together after college and our European tour. We were working on our "Mrs." degrees in Aspen.

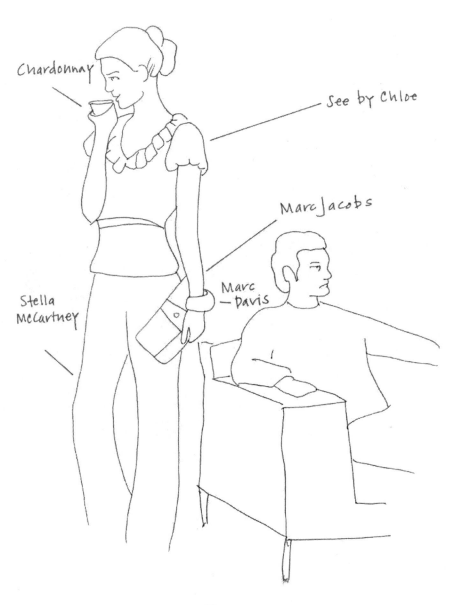

Chardonnay

See by Chloe

Marc Jacobs

Marc
—Davis

Stella
McCartney

"Without Me"

SOCIAL CLIMBERS SONGS:

Anything Classical

Uptown Girl by Billy Joel

I Want to be Rich by Calloway

High School Never Ends by Bowling For Soup

Dawn by Four- Seasons

Sweet Emotion by Aerosmith

Complicated by Avril Levine

Material Girl by Madonna

Rich Girl by Hall & Oats

Don't Be Cruel by Bobby Brown

If I was a Rich Girl by Gwen Stephani

Gold Digger by Kanye West

To Be Real by Cheryl Lynn

Real Love by Pink

Rag Doll by Four- Seasons

My Love Don't Cost a Thing by J Lo

Going Back to Cali by LL Cool Jay

Crafty by Beastie Boys (My all time favorite band!)

Cool It Now by New Edition

That Voice Again by Peter Gabriel

Lose This by Eminem

It's Tricky by Run DMC

Without Me by Eminem

Fee by Phish

Circle of Friends by REM

Breathe by Fabulous

Lucky by Britney Spears

You Don't Own Me by Lesley Gore (The First Wives Club soundtrack)

Lawyers, Guns, and Money by Warren Zevon

Lawyers in Love by Jackson Browne

Living on a thin Line by The Kinks

Fame by Irene Cara

Hey Hey What can I do by Led Zeppelin

Bust a Move by Young MC

Nasty by Janet Jackson

Naughty Girls Need Love by Samantha Fox

Mislead by Kool n the Gang

Our Lips are Sealed by The Go Gos

Jenny From The Block by J Lo

Forever in Blue Jeans by Neil Diamond

Belong by REM

If I had a Million Dollars by Barkenaked Ladies

When I grow up by Pussy Cat Girls

What a Feeling by Irene Cara

Ooops by Britney Spears

The Rose by Bette Midler

Anything by The Spice Girls (notice Posh is the only one still famous?)

Chapter XIII

PARTY, PARTY, PARTY

"It" girls go to the right parties. The day of PAS (Philadelphia Antique Show; but it is so much cuter to use initials and abbreviations), I pretend I am buying Chanel makeup and go to the department store for a free makeup application. I have makeup, but I don't really know how to apply it. I also do not want anyone to see me in Pierre and Carlo because it makes me look like I am trying too hard to look good for this event. After all, it isn't even a black tie party. It is truly a show at a convention center. For some reason opening night is a big deal. Maybe it's because the least expensive thing sold there is a million dollars. We love it and go every year.

I wear a Versace outfit (don't get too excited) from a consignment store in Atlantic City. It's one of my dirty little secrets about living at the shore and I don't want anyone to know. We all use the same stylist, Emily. She is fabulous and because of confidential clients, she has red Hermès loafers in my size. I get them used for absolutely nothing. Emily not only styles your wardrobe, she will sell your used designer clothes. So consignment shopping is my favorite. I also get my best dirt from her. Lot's of Emily's clients are selling their designer clothes to make money on the down low. She does not give out names but she has told me about one client who is selling off her wardrobe so she can eventually leave her husband. Did you know there are actually married couples that live together in separate bedrooms and hate each other but don't want anyone to know? They live like this for years to keep up appearances, and they are not even worried about their children. It's more like they are concerned what society thinks or their careers will suffer.

Anyway, I am trying on a variety of shoes with the outfit, because if I break out the Miss Trish of Capri sandals with the boats on them… well, it's still spring and that might be a little too-too.

Husband is growing impatient. "I'm writing a book," he says. I ignore all his inane comments. "It's called 'In His Shoes'," Husband laughs at himself. "Can you please decide?" Husband thinks I obsess about what to wear. I do.

"I will be down in two minutes. Will you please get me a glass of Chardonnay," I say, not asking. The phone rings. "Hello," I answer knowing I have to take Colby's call right before an event. It is probably important.

"What are you wearing?" Colby asks, sipping her martini. Yesterday Colby had a huge fight with her husband. She has had it with him. He never helps her with the children. It's her job, is what he says. Colby's pissed.

"I'm wearing Orange pants, coral Lilly pumps and an orange and, a sort-of white swirly see-through blouse." Does she have any dirt, I wonder?

"Okay, that helps. So not a cocktail dress, right?" Colby is concentrating on her closet and her martini, not our conversation.

"I didn't want to look like I was trying too hard," I add. "Husband is really rushing me. I'll see you there."

"OK, goodbye." Colby says, and I hang up.

We arrive at the event. Of course, Colby has it completely going on with her matchy white pants and über-cool Trina Turk poncho, white pants, matching bag, shoes and Gucci sunglasses. Not necessary once you are inside, but one must wear the cool sunglasses until the last possible moment. You walk in the door and then they are removed, never before. "Hi, goddess," I say giving her an air kiss; Husband gets one next. Husbands are to be ignored. We want to see what everyone is wearing, and Husband is great at fetching drinks. "Can we have wine?" I say with an "if-you-do-this-for-me-now, you-know-what-I'll-do-to-you-later" smile on my face. Husband gets the picture, so he scurries off to get drinks. Meanwhile, Colby's husband is nowhere to be found. He's probably off flirting with the bartender or looking at himself in an antique mirror.

"Look at Kitty! She is such a loser. Why is she wearing black?" Colby sneers. Black is so worn all the time, you just cannot wear it. Unless it's during the day.

"Because she is an SC, no matter who her husband is," I say back knowingly. I notice Kitty having her picture taken—again. Next to her is a cute young woman in a suit whom I have seen before but can't place. *Why is that person helping her* I wonder? Maybe she is on the committee too. I just have not met her. Just then Pippa arrives.

"Elizabeth, what are you doing here?" Pippa asks looking genuinely surprised. She is trying to be sweet. But there's a condescending tone in her voice.

"I'm on the committee," I say, wondering why the fuck she is asking me.

"Oh, it's just so far to come up for one night from the shore. Don't you have antique shows down there?" Pippa adds insult to injury. Meow! Hiss! Pippa looks like a playboy bunny, not a Pew.

Playing dumb, I say with a smile, "This is a great party, we love it and come every year. This is my third year on the committee," willing her to move on. "You should be on the committee with us next year." I say knowing she has *never* been asked. *Did I just say that?* Now I feel awful that I put her in her place. That's immature. I hate to be mean. I shouldn't be so defensive.

"You don't like your friends at the shore as much as us," Pippa says with a UB smile on her face. *How rude!*

As Pippa walks on to say hello to other friends Colby say's "What an SC," Colby stares at Pippa's back and then looks at me. *Honestly, what an insult!*

"She's just pissed that Kitty never puts her on any committees, even though they are practically neighbors. I could care less what she says to me, she's NR," I say with assuredness. If you say something like you mean it, even if you don't, everyone will believe you. I am still hurt. But I understand, no one likes to be left out.

Colby and I proceeded like that much of the night. "Hey we're the staring committee rather than the steering committee," I say cracking up with my wine buzz in check.

"Elizabeth, you are such a UB," Colby smiles in her wine haze.

"We better find Husband so I can have a cigarette and get out of here. The walls are starting to sway," I say, grabbing a drink from the bar to go with my smoke. I can't forget to tell Allegra what Pippa said to me.

Husband and I blare "Love of the common people," by Paul Young on the drive down to the shore. Note to self: *make shore friends!*

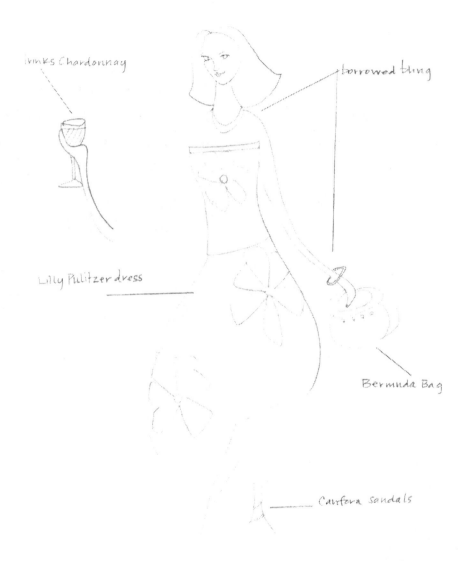

drinks Chardonnay

borrowed bling

Lilly Pulitzer dress

Bermuda Bag

Carrfora sandals

SC Cocktails:

Chardonnay (it's religious)

Madres (it's all in the name)

Kir Royale

Jack and Ginger

Spiced Rum and Diet Coke

Serendipities (The Ritz, Paris)

Light Beer

Margaritas (hit the hard stuff but make it look froo froo)

Dirty Martini

Cosmo (because SCs are so cosmopolitan)

Champagne (it just looks fancy)

Vodka Gimlet

Scotch (because if you know what a malt is, you are chic)

Gin and Tonic

Half and Half (the ultimate country club drink)

Bloody Mary

Bellini

Mojito

Chapter XIV

How To Be Wasp

"It" girls always look put together; effortlessly put together. The next week, Allegra and I meet for manicures and pedicures. When I first met Allegra she was a Catholic (no pre-marital sex or birth control) Democrat (lots of taxes for poor people). Now she is a converted Episcopalian Republican—just like me (Allegra doesn't have a lot of sympathy for poor people—I know she will be more understanding once she finds a husband)! Afterward, we eat at Hymie's Deli. Even though it is in the Waspy-ist Village on the Main Line (Gladwyne), every WASP likes a good Jewish Deli. Allegra looks fabulous as always, sporting a simple black shift, with cap sleeves, huge black pearl earrings and quadruple-strand black pearls all twisted together, and a matching bracelet. Carefully placed on her right hand index finger is a large black pearl ring. She has patent Jimmy Choo stilettos', "Adele" style with gold, diamond and black onyx chain across the toe. "It" girls have the best jewelry and shoes to boot. Her jewelry always distracts me. While we drink our tomato juice and eat our matzo ball soup, Allegra is relating to me the trials and tribulations of her love affair. My friends know to never talk to me about their sex lives. I mean, come on, I am a married women. What do I know about sex?

Allegra was seeing this guy Frank: "For the first couple of weeks he called all the time and then just stopped. I just don't get it," Allegra says.

Not being part of the game makes me secretly glad that I am married. I mean, when Field is throwing a temper tantrum over the fact that I sliced his toast in half and he wanted it whole and all that stuff, then I start to miss my single life. I miss my single days because I had no responsibilities, and sometimes wish that I could jet off with Allegra on her next trip to San Tropez. Being a parent is exhausting. But, really, if you are not Mrs. Quinn, how can you be on all of these committees? Dr. and Mrs. Quinn looks so much better on an invitation than just Elizabeth Mitchell.

I am a really good listener, and I tell Allegra my standard advice, "Don't worry, you'll meet somebody, you are gorgeous", which she is, "and perfect," which she is, and "he will 'pick you'." "Just go out as much as possible and they 'pick you'," I console. Here's the little thing about men that I always tell my single friends: "Allegra, you will always date all of the wrong men until you meet the perfect man, and then you date the right one and you realize that he is the one that you want to marry." I think that it is as simple as that. Okay, here's my thing about dating.

"Let's here your theory again, Elizabeth," Allegra says, stirring more pepper into her tomato juice. She thinks it raises her metabolism. Being single makes our conversations very one sided. We talk about love a lot. Her lack of it, not mine.

"They always 'pick you'. I know you want to pick them, but there is no real point because they always 'pick you', at least, if you are happy. I mean, I know plenty of delusional people that are married or dating men that they think they picked. If they did indeed pick them, I can assure you that they will not end up being married for long. That is what happened to me when I was looking for Husband. You don't want to marry the guy you see across the room that you think is so hot. It is completely unrealistic, and you are setting yourself up for a miserable marriage." I continue my lecture as Allegra stares at her soup. This is what I love about my married friends. None of us are happy all the time or completely in love or talking about our husbands 24/7. It is merely status quo. "You marry a 1/3 nerd who is completely infatuated with you, thinks you are beautiful, buys you pretty jewelry, and doesn't get mad at you. It is so much better than getting your heart all torn up about some hot guy," I continue. That is why it always makes total sense to me that Mommie, Grandmother and Colby married their third love. "I met Husband at a dinner dance. He had been told about me. He just loved me at first sight. We have been together since I was 23. Husband 'picked me'. And that is my dating theory!" I finally finish. Husband told me he knew he had to marry me because I was the first girlfriend he had who he missed. He can't stand to be away from me. *Isn't that cute!*

"I know," says Allegra. She still looks hurt. "Are you going to the Union League happy hour?" Allegra asks, changing the subject.

"Yes, I believe I'll stop by," I say, trying to cheer her up. "Did you hear that they are trying to black-ball Merritt from joining?"

"No, that's ridiculous, she's so sweet! Why?" Allegra asks, while paying the bill.

"I have no idea. Nor do I really care. What's ironic is the person who's doing it isn't even from Philadelphia! Where do they get off!" Main Liners are very territorial. If you are from here, it allows more leeway. If you are not, you should bite your tongue and try to fit in, not ostracize people from clubs. But I know Allegra doesn't care about Merritt's club memberships.

As we walk to our cars, a huge black Lexus SUV speeds by. I can't help but notice it is Kitty on her cell phone. What is even more annoying is her license plate. MLKITTY. She is wearing her Lilly Pulitzer tennis whites, a cute top and skirt I have seen her wear many a time. It has pink and green piping. I am sure she is off to her lesson at the Merion Cricket Club, and tennis whites are required but she gets away with the pink and green piping because her last name is Kimmel. Really, who does she think she is?!

"What does that mean?" Allegra asks in horror, referring to her license plate.

"Main Line Kitty," I say slowly for effect.

"Ugh!" We both roll our eyes.

"What an SC" Allegra adds as I smile. Kitty is unbelievably tacky.

"I heard she's pulling Merritts' recommendation to be a member at The Merion Cricket Club," I say. Poor Merritt, must not be playing by the rules. I wonder what she did? Her husband is a bit crazy when he drinks. I think it's funny.

"Wow. Two clubs. She isn't doing a good job as an SC," says Allegra, not really caring.

"Because Merritt didn't help her get the girls into Tarlton." Mimi tells me everything. I always get the best dirt from Mimi!

"Oh, that's a shame," Allegra says sarcastically.

Kitty sure has secured a place for herself in society, I think. Meeting Kit Kimmel is the best thing that ever happened to Kitty. After we left college she moved home right away. No one could really figure out why, but at that point, I did not care as I had seen way too much of Kitty for the last 16 years. "It" girls travel after college, not go home and work. Scott-free, I moved to Colorado to ski, while Kitty went home. The way I hear it is they met at a bar. Kit is from The Main Line but had gone to Deerfield for boarding school and then Princeton. So they never had met before. Kit was engaged at the time, but Kitty was smitten. Kit belonged to every club in town, and came from one of the most prestigious families from Philadelphia-New York City retail legacy (Barneys). Kitty sank her claws into Kit and got him to break off his engagement, moving in right away. She made sure that poor fiancé of Kit's found out he was secretly seeing Kitty. It was as if he never had a chance. You would think he wouldn't want a wife named Kitty since his nickname is Kit. His real name is Harry Kitrell Kimmel. Rumor has it she was seeing someone else, but no one knows whom. Obviously, she couldn't have cared less, since she dropped him for a better guy. That became his problem. And Kit married an SC. By the time we all got back from Aspen she was engaged, and none of us were invited to the wedding. Whatever! She played the "low-key" bride. Said the wedding was for family only. She did not want a fuss or anything in the papers. Boy that's changed! I always wonder why, because she had acted like such a queen when we were growing up. Once they were married, they had a small reception at The Union League (one of the Kimmel's clubs) with 200 people in attendance. Mostly Kit's friends and family from what I've heard. And then, we all got kind of wrapped up in our engagements/weddings/pregnancies *et al*, but now we are all friendly again, at least for committee purposes. That's how it goes on the Main Line.

Shit! I think as I drive home. I forgot to tell Allegra about Pippa. "No Sleep Till Brooklyn," blares by the Beastie Boys. All those black pearls Allegra was wearing confused me. I lose my train of thought around her jewelry.

Vineyard Vines

Ralph
Lauren blazer

Lilly
Pulitzer

Vineyard Vines Belt

Brooks Brothers

Gucci

Kate
Spade

SOCIAL CLIMBERS STORIES/BOOKS:

Bobos

Essentially Lily (There is only one Lily Pulitzer, so a AT would never dream of trying to entertain like her.)

Class

The Social Registrar

Happy Times

Pride & Prejudice (Jane Austen wrote the original SC books)

Bonfire of The Vanities

A Man in Full

Bergdorf Blondes

The Right Address

Trading Up

Emily Post

The Devil Wears Prada

Great Gatsby

Brave New World

Who's Who (it is pay to play)

Miss Manners

Vanity Fair

Gone With The Wind

The Debutante Divorcée

Bright Young Things

Any Biography about Jackie O

Chapter XV

The Importance Of The Right Table

Having the perfect seat at a restaurant is extremely important to SCs. ATs prefer them too if they are single like Allegra. Capitol Grille is a see and be seen restaurant. Frank and Allegra used to cocktail there frequently. Allegra knows the hostess and called ahead to make sure we had the best seat. One cannot act like one care's once in the restaurant. That's pathetic. I doubt Allegra steels from Capitol Grille. I am wearing a crisp white Anne Fontaine blouse and a yellow pencil skirt from J. Crew. I was just across the street, at Pierre & Carlo, where Peter blew my hair out. Allegra is stunning in Dolce & Gabbana pants and great Guiseppe Zanotti shoes. We are meeting to specifically analyze the Pippa comment at PAS. "She had never gone before," I explain to Allegra as we sip wine and ignore our food. "Now that she is married, the Pew's practically underwrite the entire event." Another sip. "But Kitty did not put her on the committee, and I have been on it every year." I stop.

"What did she say?" Asks Allegra while smoothing her golden brown hair.

"She asked me why I was there and then proceeded to say don't you have antique shows in Atlantic City you could go to. Like I don't belong. Or was not good enough to be there. It was rude." Another sip "to top it off she walked away saying you just prefer your main line friends. Like, I don't have cool friends at the shore." Which I don't but I am planning on changing that this summer at the yacht club. I am going to be friends with people from the shore, now!

"Elizabeth, Pippa may well be married but the circumstances are less than ideal." Allegra says supportively. "Plus, you do prefer us," Allegra smiles.

"Agreed. Mimi told me that Britta, Pippa's sister-in-law does not like her." Another sip.

"I'm sure her in-laws don't like her either, she broke up their son's first marriage. Plus, there were children involved." True statement. I was just so happy that Pippa got married; I believed the first marriage was doomed. No matter what Kitty says.

"Pippa did always want to be the first married and the first one to have children." I add.

"And you certainly took home that trophy. So MC," Allegra laughs.

"It does not help that I am on a lot of committees and she is not. Plus, the tea group." I sigh, feeling guilty about what I said to her that night. *She provoked me!*

"Chalk it up to jealousy and insecurity. She's NR. If you're really worried ask Mimi. She knows her best." Allegra glances at a wealthy businessman who just walked in wearing a breath taking custom suit.

I shake my head no, no, "They 'pick you' remember?"

Allegra sighs, "So what are the summer plans?" Allegra is over the conversation. Change the subject.

"Mommie and I go to Waterloo Gardens to get our salmon colored plants. Also I am planning the big summer party for The Ocean City Yacht Club. Will you please come?" I like having Allegra by my side. She gives me more confidence. Maybe she will meet a man from the shore. Then we can live next door to one another as we always planned to in college.

"Yes, I'll go. Just email me the date so I can put in on my calendar." Allegra sort of groans. "Can I go with you and Mommie to Waterloo?" Allegra will make Fran plant her plants. But she would never dream of letting her pick them out.

Chapter XVI

THE OCEAN CITY YACHT CLUB

Although no one envy's the fact that I live at the shore, once summer arrives every single person I know summers here. Except Pippa, Pew's go to Maine. WASPy Mimi's shore house is in The Gardens, Ocean City. Colby's Irish Catholic, so therefore in Long Port. The Kimmel's own a beachfront mansion in Ventnor. We all belong to The Ocean City Yacht Club. Since Husband sails there I got roped into planning the summer party. Navy Blue Blazers are required after 5:00 P.M. at the club. I am throwing a preppy party. It is so much easier to dress for since I am in Lilly Pulitzer from Memorial Day to Labor Day. I'm not kidding.

Allegra comes to my house to get ready for the party. Nana has the boys in the pool so we have the house to ourselves. Being bombarded with questions from Greye and Field is a serious distraction when one is picking out jewelry. "If I were King for just one day," by the Thompson Twins plays on my iPhone

"Mommie is so funny," Allegra is applying mascara.

"I know. She's on another planet." I am staring at my wood trunk full of jewelry. Mommie tried to get it in New York City for me when I turned 16. It is mahogany with my initials on a brass plate on the top. It's glamorous. Mommie ended up buying it in Philadelphia at J.E.Caldwell & Co.

When Allegra and I met Mommie at Waterloo Gardens she was waiting for us in their café sipping diet coke and reading *The Suburban*.

"I've never seen someone actually read the society pages before." Allegra has moved onto putting bronzing powder all over her body.

"When I lived in Zimbabwe she mailed it to me every week," I laugh. Poor tree huggers. I was such a shock to the system. Even though I was in Africa I still wore Laura Ashley. Not Birkenstock. "One of the other students I was with told me they didn't believe society pages even really existed." Too funny! I'm so glad I was there to educate them on the society page.

Allegra walks out of the bathroom to find me laying out my jewelry. A charm bracelet with a white bee on it. Matching necklace, bee earrings and a bee ring. I love summer. I don't have to go to The Main Line all the time. Everyone is here. "You are just like my Grandmother. She always arranges her things that way. She has a jewelry box just like that." *Nice compliment!*

I would love to be wealthy like that, 300 million dollars wealthy and hide it in Monaco. And have a title, to be royal and have people kiss my ass. I would have a butler too and love meeting Queens. SS is so nice. I wouldn't have to put up with the UB. I would have fancy JP Tod's driving shoes, like Allegra's Grandmother, just for driving my navy blue (the only acceptable color according to her Grandmother) Lancia with suede interior. She probably has a driver now.

"Don't you look cute in your Pucci shift," I admire. Allegra does not do preppy. It's so MC of us. But, rumor has it Allegra has been spotted at Van Cleve—a very traditional women's clothing store in Paoli. "Will you greet at the door of the club while I finish setting up?"

"Sure, I will wait for Mimi and Colby." Allegra grabs her clutch. Poor Allegra. Husband is my purse at parties. He carries my cigarettes, lighter, lipstick and iPhone.

"Remember what Mommie said?" I ask on our way to the car. We have a driver tonight with a black Lincoln Town Car. Husband will meet us at the club. He is seeing post-ops in the Ocean City office.

"Of course," Allegra lightly laughs. When we met Mommie at Waterloo Gardens she looked up from her newspaper and exclaimed, "Look at you girls! You always dress like you are going to a cocktail party." Allegra was wearing a Missoni dress and wedge heels.

And Allegra said, "Mommie, our life *is* one big cocktail party."

"Well we are certainly living up to our reputation!" I say feeling so confident and chic. Everyone calls my mother Mommie. Even some of her friends do it too.

Once at The Ocean City Yacht Club I situate Allegra at the door with a Pink Lilly. I did the entire party in pink and green. Even the drinks are pink with a mint sprig. The Pink Lilly is rum, pineapple and grapefruit juice, and a splash of grenadine to make it pink. I have pink and green: balloons, table clothes, napkins, chair covers, and plates, plastic dinnerware, place cards—you name it! It's such a cute party. I put plastic pink flamingos all along the front lawn of the club, they offset the green grass perfectly. We hired a Neil Diamond impersonator to sing. There are two kinds of people in this world. Those who love Neil Diamond, and those who don't. I really didn't mind being on the committee. Committees are playgroups for grown ups. And now that I am determined to make shore friends, this is a step in the right direction. Plus, you get to get dressed up. I have outdone myself this time. Mimi and Colby will Love it.

The deck of the club is on the bay. I decide to put a pitcher of Pink Lilly's on every table as everyone begins to arrive. I even have a Lilly Pulitzer beach blanket down to look like a rug. The devil is in the details and I am putting my best foot forward for my shore friends. I can see Kitty at the front door. She's not ruining my night. I grab a drink off the bar and walk inside to rescue Allegra. "Hi, Kitty, How are you?" I ask.

"Great! We just got down last night. We were at the Grahams annual summer party." Kitty is looking over my shoulder to see if there is anyone better to talk to. That is so tacky by the way. If you are at a party just say so. Don't drop the name. Sometimes it is okay to be vague. Then you are not hiding something but rather not name-dropping. Like, "We saw each other last Saturday and..." vs. "We were at Radnor Hunt and..."

"I love your dress," I compliment. It looks Bill Blass but I will never dare ask. If I got it wrong she will crucify me at an Academy Ball meeting.

"Loewe. I just love their clothes." Kitty smiles like the UB she is. *WHO?*

AT Allegra saves the day "Did you go to Madrid to buy the clothes?" She knows the brand and can prove it.

"Yes. Allegra I've been meaning to talk to you. You work. I am thinking about selling something. You know like Arbonne." She changed the subject. Interesting. *Why does she want to work?* I wouldn't become an Avon lady so I could buy Dior.

"I sell jewelry to jewelry stores. Not at parties in people's houses in the evening," Allegra purrs in her accent. *Playing the snob card. Smart.* Allegra always stick up for me.

Colby and Mimi arrive screaming "Elizabeth! We love this party theme. It is so cute! What are these drinks?" They called to wish me good luck in the morning. They always cheer me on. I love Colby and Mimi.

"The Pink Lilly. I can email the recipe." I say proudly smiling. I knew it would be a hit. I see the staff butlering the drinks in pink and green cups. I met with the Chef and staff before hand during their prep. From my experience in PR one can never be too detailed oriented. The waiters are wearing pink izod shirts and kelly green shorts.

Colby and Mimi air kiss us all. "It is so good, and you know I don't drink this sweet shit," Mimi laughs.

"What do you think Kitty?" Colby turns.

"Um hm, I love to party," Kitty would never dream of complimenting me, or anyone else for that matter. *UB!*

Allegra touches my arm "The Yacht Club people want you in a picture out front. I totally forgot I was supposed to get you."

"I'll be back," I say turning to go out front. First time Kitty isn't being photographed and I am. I might be fitting in better down here.

After dinner we all sit outside to smoke. Kitty has left, thankfully. Up walks an unfamiliar face. "Mimi!" She calls out.

"America," by Neil Diamond plays in the background.

"Oh my God! Beth I haven't seen you in forever," Mimi jumps up and gives her a big hug.

Colby and Allegra start gossiping and ignoring the Beth person.

"Beth you have to meet Elizabeth, she did the party." Mimi beams as I get up to go over and meet Beth. I am tired and just want to relax.

"Hi, Nice to meet you. Do you live in Ocean City?" I say with a big smile, trying to get my conversation mojo going. It is nice to ask questions and not talk about yourself the whole time like fucking Kitty.

Beth just sort of stares at me "No. We live in Haddonfield. Do you?" She looks blankly at me as if I am boring her.

"Yes, we live in Margate." I say with as much confidence as I can muster. As I finish I notice her staring at my engagement ring. And then she quickly looks away.

"Oh. Mimi have you been back on the Main Line during the year?" Beth just shut me down. She is obviously more interested in reconnecting with her old friend who she seems to be soooo impressed with. Wonder how they know one another. Haddonfield is a fancy town in New Jersey, outside of Philadelphia. I am confident Mimi has never been there.

"Yes but I'm engaged, I am getting married next summer in Manchester." Mimi says.

"Then you must visit me in Dorset!" Beth clings to Mimi. They must have gone to summer camp together--Oneka. It's in Vermont. And she seems well aware of who Mimi's family is. Total SC! I just walk away and sit back down with Allegra and Colby.

"Is your dress Vanessa Fox?" Beth squeals as she practically rips Mimi's dress trying to look for the tag. *SC!*

Instead I say, "So what's the dirt from tonight?"

"Kitty was telling Mimi that the only thing men are good for is money. And women are for sex and laundry." Colby is laughing.

"Was she drunk?" What a weird thing to say.

"I doubt it, she is demented." Colby inhales her cigarette.

"She told me she is not friends with Bently anymore." Says Allegra. Bently was one of her best friends.

"I wonder who dropped who?" This is a good one.

"Don't get mad," Allegra prepares me.

"Why, what?" I am feeling pressure in my chest.

"Promise you aren't going to freak out here? You can do it in the car." Allegra demands.

"Okay, Promise. Tell me!" I demand back.

"When Kitty arrived she asked where you were. I said out back and she said probably with a bottle of wine." Allegra looks amused but is trying to read my face.

"UB! I was setting up the tables." She does not like that I am on a committee that didn't include her.

"Don't say anything, it's not worth it." Allegra is being stern. I hate when she tells me what to do.

"I won't." I mean it.

The next day Beth called me at home to ask if her Father could see Husband. He needs eye surgery. Apparently he lives at the shore. She was soooo nice. Typical. Mimi probably told her about us, she Googled our name, and found that article. Of course, I gave her the office phone number. I only personally call when it is for Allegra, Colby, Mimi or Pippa.

Chapter XVII

How One Summers At The Shore

"It" girls love the beach. The Quinn's' go to the beach every Sunday. Since we live on the bay we go to the Osborne Avenue beach club. They have showers. I am wearing my Lilly Pulitzer pink and green bikini and the boys have matching swimsuit trunks. Husband allows me to put us all is matching bathing suits. He is just happy to sit, read and do nothing on the beach. Osborne Avenue is where we had our beach portrait taken. I used it that year as my Christmas card. It was very pretty.

Greye is trying to surf and we dig Field a big hole so he can sit in it. I packed the cooler with tons of Corona Lights and limes. The boys already had lunch. It is a sunny, clear, perfect day to sit under an umbrella and relax. As we set up our chairs (also pink) and lay our towels over them (green), Sue Smith saunters over. She has on a black and white checked bikini with a bow. Her hair is pulled back with an oversized black silk scarf. Sue looks very sophisticated. I pull my white izod sunglasses from my head to my eyes and sit down. "Hi!" I say so she can hear me. *I am making shore friends.*

"Hi, what have you been up to?" Sue's sweet.

"Give a little love," by Ziggy Marley plays on my iPhone.

"Want a beer?" I ask opening my corona light with a beer opener shaped like a fish and put it in my pink and green monogrammed cup holder. It is from Vera Bradley so it only has a Q embroidered.

"Sure," Sue says as she sits down next to me right into the sand. *What a women!* I would never want sand all over my butt.

"We're good. We've been boating a lot. You should come with us next time." I suggest. *See how good I am at keeping my goals and making shore friends.*

"We'd love to. Any night is good." Sue takes a sip of beer.

"Husband," I call, "What night should the Smith's meet us on the boat?" I ask.

"Whenever," Husband does not handle our social calendar. I do.

"How about tomorrow?" I throw out there.

"Perfect, what time." Sue's husband is nice and her children go to school with Greye. Sue's family owns the Margate Bridge, along with a lot of other things. She is on the board of the local hospital. There's money in New Jersey. Rich people at the shore just like to act like farmers. I can't get into that mentality. They are WASPier than The Main Line. I'm not into people seeing me in my yoga pants. You know I'm having a nervous breakdown if I'm out running errands in work out clothes.

"Five o'clock," Husband is usually home by four.

"Great, what should I bring?" Sue asks.

"Sandwiches," I suggest. I don't cook, but I always have plenty of wine.

"I'll get them from the Cheese Board. What do you guys like?" Sue asks.

"Anything. Please make mine a vegetarian." I really need to lose the last few baby pounds. I am moving onto eating vegetables only. Hopefully that will work.

"Okay," Sue chuckles, "What about the boys?"

"Turkey, ham, anything really. We are really easy," because they have to be. We like to water ski so our boat is only 21 feet long. It is a Boston Whaler. I love it! It is blue and white.

"All right then. See you tomorrow at five o'clock," Sue stands up and starts to wipe of the sand on her butt.

"I'll have all the drinks we could possibly want. Beer, wine, soda, water and juice boxes for the children." I am a good hostess; I just think the kitchen is too hot when the oven's on. My hair could frizz.

Field is eating the sand off his hands when Sue reappears. "Elizabeth I want you to meet Lisa and Denise." Trailing behind Sue are two cute girls—both blond.

"Hi," I say standing up. "Nice to meet you." I shake both their hands. "This is my Husband." I point to Husband who has not spoken once since we got here. He loves to read and not talk. I'm a talker.

After Husband shakes both their hands and sits back down I begin to grill "Lisa did you grow up here?"

"Yes, in Linwood. But I went away for school." *Where? I like when people don't name drop.*

"I went to Lake Forest College, everyone was from a boarding school." I throw it out there so she will play the name game. Then I can find out what school. See how good I am at getting information without being pushy.

"Oh did you know Mandy Masterson?" Lisa's eyes are bright with curiosity.

"Yes! I love Mandy, she was in my sorority but a year below me." Bingo she went to Pomfret in Connecticut. *That's impressive.*

"What about you Denise?" I smile at her.

"I went to Holy Spirit. My husband was a lifeguard in Ocean City." I know all about the Life Guard Mafia at the shore. Husband was one too.

"Then my husband would know him," I say loudly so Husband can hear me. Denise walks over to ask.

"I hope I see you here again soon," I say goodbye dying to find out what their families do for a living.

Chapter XVIII

PREPPY PEOPLE BOAT

"It" girls know how to sail and drive a motorboat. I, however, can do neither. I enjoy the ride, scenery and sit on my butt. I do have a pink kayak. Today the Smith's are coming on the boat.

My landscaper is outside laying down dirt and mulch. I am having pac-a-sandra laid on the side of my yard. I used to let the lawn have a natural look but honestly it was filled with weeds and looked like shit. I have my salmon colored plants in pots around the deck, down the stairs and around the pool. But the side of my yard, that I rarely see needs help. Naturescapes is helping me get my act together. Mommie is an avid gardener. I am not. I want the house to look pretty, so I hire people. I have on Miss Trish of Capri sandals with a sailboat as the thong. I have on a navy blue miracle suit that is strapless. Sue's Jetta pulls into the driveway. I like Volkswagens, but I think they are geared towards teenagers not debutantes.

I greet at the door, "Hello! Welcome." I call out as the Smiths get out of the car.

"Thank you so much for having us," Sue's husband says as they enter the house.

"They're here," I call to Husband. Greye and Field match their father in navy blue board shorts from J.Crew.

As we walk down to the dock I am proud to show the Smith's our view. Husband starts the engine once we are all on and "I never," by the Killers plays on the radio.

"This is a great house," Sue compliments.

"Thanks. We love it," I sit in the back seat so I can put my feet on the side of the boat and see the view. *Maybe I'll have a summer party.* I had highball and high heels one year. It was really fun, but we usually do our parties in the fall when the traffic isn't as awful. Summer is nuts here. Girls just wanna have rum was my best party. I actually rented the margarita man's big drink machines, put up palm trees and served drinks out of plastic coconut cups.

After water skiing we dock at a private beach and get out the food. "I've never been to Spain," by Three Dog Night plays on the radio. After Sue serves her children she comes back to sit with me. In a lady like way she puts one leg over the side of the boat. So she is straddling the boat. She looks chic. This comes naturally to her, I can tell. "Do you do any charity work at the shore?" Sue asks.

I'm really fitting in nicely, I think. "I do. Why?"

"I'm on the board of Shore Memorial Hospital and we are looking for some new blood. Young blood. Eventually most members will be gone. I'm the only one under 60."

I know. "I do a ton of stuff in Philadelphia. My schedule is crazy. I'd be on a committee for now. Can I think about The Board?" I can't bite off more than I can chew. Kitty will kill me if I don't dazzle her with raffles.

"Perfect. We have an event this fall," Sue is sweet to include me. I knew I'd meet more shore friends.

"I'm thinking of having a Labor Day party. Does anyone else? I'd like to invite some of the families from The Beach Club." I don't want to have a loser event no one can come to. That would suck.

"We're free," say Sue breezily. Sue has on a Gottex bathing suit with a nautical print. Very yacht appropriate. Except our boat is not a yacht. "You should bring the boys to our pool club one evening. It's fun." Sue adds.

I know all about this "pool club," Sue belongs to. It is ridiculous. They say the membership is closed. Will not even accept application. I've never seen anything like it. This is what rubs me the wrong way about the shore. You have to "know" someone to get in. In reality you need to know about five people and even then your not secured a spot. The "pool club" is not even fancy. I could care less as I have my own pool! "Yes that would be lovely," I say instead. I'm still trying to make friends. On the Main Line people are dying to get into golf clubs where the U.S. Open is held not a mini YMCA. *So gay!*

" I really liked Lisa and Denise." I am gearing up to get the dirt. "Do they work?" I ask innocently.

"Denise's parents own the salt water taffy company in Atlantic City." Sue pauses and sips wine, "She does not work there but her husband does. Lisa's father is a judge and owns a law firm in Atlantic City. Her in laws own the Atlantic City Country Club." *Sweet! Free candy and golf lessons for the boys.* The Atlantic City Country Club has the best crab cakes! Sue shares more, my kind of girl. "Lisa is a teacher and also on city council."

"Wow! That's a lot. How many children does she have?" I don't think I could handle all of that.

"Three. All boys. She has a staff." Sue sort of smirks.

"She must! We should all go to The Chelsea for dinner." *More shore friends!* The Chelsea is a new boutique hotel in Atlantic City right on the beach. It's chic.

"Indeed. I will set it up." Sue is the queen bee of Atlantic City.

"Great. Thanks, let me know." I say. I love being on the water. It makes me happy. Probably something to do with the fact that I'm a cancer. Crabs need water—*bla, bla, bla.*

"Maybe we'll get a boat," Sue smiles over at her husband who is getting a tour of the dashboard from Husband. Husband is sexy. I love to watch him drive and he is one of the best water skiers I have ever seen! Husband had a sailboat and motorboat when he grew up. I can't stand having to switch sides and possibly be hit in the head with the boom. No sailboats for us.

Chapter XIX

SUNDAYS

Planning continues for the Academy Ball and another meeting is scheduled for tomorrow. Today, I am sitting in my kitchen, doing my favorite Sunday thing, cutting out coupons. This, by the way, is a huge secret that I do not want people to know. I love cutting coupons. The idea of saving 50 cents on something just makes me happy! It feels as good as when I buy new Kate Spade shoes (granted, I wish I could afford to only buy Jimmy Choos but...). Like I earned it. Don't get me wrong. I'm happier when I buy Pierre Deux instead of Vera Bradley. Nonetheless, I like to save money on grocery items. Remember, cutting coupons is embarrassing, makes me look poor and no one must know about it.

I have a cup of French press coffee. I know I'm supposed to drink green tea, but I can't help it. I buy Dunkin' Donuts hazelnut coffee and use a sugar-free hazelnut creamer. It is divine! I prefer sugar-free, something about sugar breaking down your collagen sounds like it would age me, yuck. Since I have a committee meeting tomorrow morning, I must remember to get everything done, such as making my phone calls. I need to contact The Four Seasons, The Ritz Carlton, Jacques Ferber, Craig Drake and everyone that I can--trying to get raffle gifts. I want to be sure that I am doing my part on the raffle committee this year and that I come through with really amazing gifts. I need to appear to be a truly excellent committee member. Of course, all I care about is access to Oscar.

On Monday I need to go to my dermatologist. I have rosacia, and I always go to my dermatologist to get my glycolic peels—50% every four weeks. I feel that there are certain things that you must do on a maintenance level (no sugar), and you need to prepare for them. I went to etiquette school, so I have rules:

You always say pardon me, please, and thank you. If you don't hear someone, don't say "what", say "pardon me." You always get a manicure and pedicure every week. Eyebrows should be waxed and dyed every month. Your eyebrows should be a shade darker than your hair. It's all about the contrast. Never poo or pee with the door open. Husbands don't need to hear that. I get my hair trimmed every six weeks. I get a massage every month and a facial directly afterward. I get a scrub every eight weeks and do my own exfoliation weekly. I bleach my teeth once a year at my birthday to look younger. Stand up straight. My trainer has an exercise we do every week just to improve my posture. It makes you look thinner and more serious. You get more respect. I put fresh flowers in my bedroom, my entrance hall and my kitchen. Fresh flowers denote nature and help you be in a positive mood, which is important. Always accept compliments. Say "Thank you," instead of "no way." Always say "yes," instead of "yeah." It simply sounds nicer. Be articulate. Say what you mean. When you mean no, say no, and don't complain. I can't stand complainers. (Note to self: *stop complaining.*) Change something you don't like instead of complaining about it. It is that simple. You should always try to remember not to worry about petty things. You should be thankful instead for your health, your children, and the good health of your family and friends. Don't change your plans, or be late. I see that as a weakness. Write thank you notes and return all calls; don't hide behind email. Don't wear jeans. Those are my rules.

Husband says I am controlling, I like to think I'm organized. Greye's friend once told me I was bossy. I can be short tempered. I hate to yell it ages me. But it's hard living with all boys. My theory is its Gods little trick on me. Since my parents were divorced and I went to an all girls school, I am not used to living with men. Even in college, I lived with my sorority sisters. Men can be so messy. They throw their clothes everywhere and get pee on the toilet seat. Men are smellier too. I don't want to lose my temper. Colby says it is our job as parents to keep our children in line. She yells constantly. I'm not perfect either. I have never once cleaned my own house. I have no idea how to turn on our stereo and I can't reach the light bulbs (I have high ceilings). My little gentlemen help me. I need them. Greye has even learned to hold the door for me. Husband handles the car doors. So In any case, I must work on my raffle.

"Hello, is Anne Kelly available?" I ask the receptionist as hotel staff works weekends. "Anne, it's Elizabeth Quinn. How are you?" I say politely.

"Hi, Elizabeth, are you calling about your tea?" Anne asks.

"No, I think we are set with the menu and cocktails. I wanted to see if the Rittenhouse would be willing to donate an overnight stay and dinner for Academy Ball?" It isn't that hard to get donations for this event. You simply ask the people you already do business with. They want to keep you happy, customer service. It's a tax write off for them. Everyone gives to charity. I am experienced in asking for things. I had to ask a lot of writers and producers to talk about my clients when I did PR.

"Of course. Just fax or mail me the form and I will give you the certificate next time you're in the hotel." Anne is very professional. I like working with her.

"Great, thank you so much, Anne," I say, feeling accomplished.

I have my committee meeting the next day. I need to plan for my turn to host the tea. Since I would never dream of cooking, my tea will be held at The Rittenhouse Hotel. I always have a tea properly at a hotel, not cutting tea sandwiches at my house. Shit! Note to self: *call Ann back, and plan Mimi's bridal shower.* Plus, I am planning a terrific gift bag to wow everyone. I have bath bombs, lotion and face mask samples from Lush, a copy of *Main Line Magazine*, a note pad and pencil from Details, a long-stemmed rose, Keihl's samples and drinks for two at The Ritz Bar!

Husband is yelling in the living room over a pre-season Eagles game. Don't get me wrong; I love football, and particularly the Eagles, but he gets so heated about it. Plus it is still entirely too hot to watch football. I'm not ready yet. "WHAT! NOOOOOOOOOOOOO!

You should be fired!" Husband screams at the TV. I pour myself a glass of wine, open a beer for Husband and walk into the living room to join him before I head up for my Sunday afternoon bath. The boys have pulled every toy Nana put away out onto the floor. And Fields bottle of milk is seeping into my oriental carpet. *This mess!* My bath will sooth me.

Upstairs I light my candles and close my door. I turn on the iPhone. "I want to be your lover, lover boy," by Bill Ocean plays. I grab *Chasing Harry Winston* off my nightstand and pick up the phone. Closing the bathroom door, in combination with the bedroom door and music, I won't be disturbed. Once the bath is running and full of floral scent salts, oils and bubbles I put my hair up. Then the torturous exfoliation begins. Immersed in the bath I apply a collagen facemask and lay back on the bath pillow. Deep breathing, in through the nose out through the mouth. That gets rid of stale air. In through nose out through the nose. That is detox breathing. Yoga helps me stay zen. As I marinate in flowers I contemplate what to wear. I visualize my closet, Red Kate Spade boardwalk dress, perfect. Maybe we can take the boys out for dinner on the boat. I like docking at the restaurant and walking up to eat. It feels so islandy to me. I sip my wine and open my book. This takes my mind off everything. I'll pretend I'm in Bali.

Social Climber's Closet:

Lilly Pulitzer

Tretorns

Wolford

Asprey

Anya Hindmarch

Talbot's sunglasses ($50 vs. $500)

Hidalgo pastel rings

A puss on their face

Jack Rogers Shoes—customized, of course

Pearls

Albright Inc Fashion Library (if you can't afford the real thing rent it)

Izod

Bad Attitudes

Rupert Sanderson shoes & luggage

Diamonds

Jennifer Miller Jewelry

Cartier

Tiffany & Co

Borrowed Bling (you can borrow jewelry for a fee)

Fake personalities

Pastel-colored necklaces and matching earrings (which match their cashmere sweater sets)

J. McLaughlin printed pants (JM)

JM custom bags with your zip code (90210 vs. 19087)

C J Laing

Gold charm bracelets

Kenneth Jay Lane (why buy real when you can pull off the fake stuff)

Amy Jo Gladstone needlepoint or monogrammed slippers

Canfora sandals

Rosa Cha bathing suits

Anything tortoise-shell

Belgium loafers

Harold's

A wall so no one really knows who they are

Signet rings

Hermès Beach Towels

K Swiss

Globe Trotter Luggage

Shrimp rings

Vanessa Fox dresses

Anything from Van Cleve

Hermès scarves

Needlepoint Bermuda Bags

Bag Borrow or Steal (YSL bags starting at $60 a week)

Lots and lots of skeletons!!!!

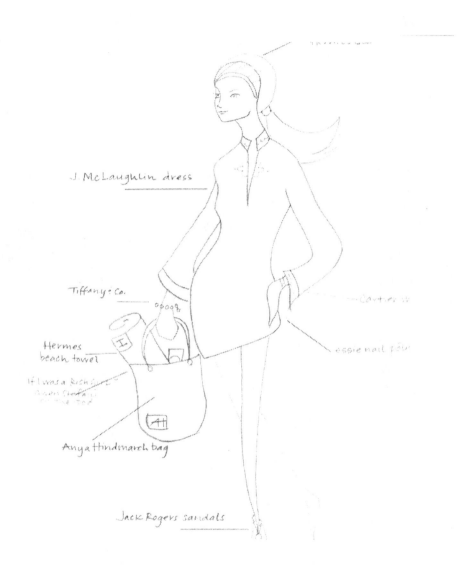

J. McLaughlin dress

Tiffany & Co.

Hermes
beach towel

If I was a Rich Girl
poem stanza
on the top

Anya Hindmarch bag

Jack Rogers sandals

Cartier

essie nail 760

14.

Chapter XX

LIFE'S A BEACH

"It" girls are fabulous entertainers. I decided not to have my party on Labor Day. I'm having it a bit earlier because *everyone* has a Labor Day party. I sent out post card invitations with a light brown colored shell at the top. Directly under it read in light brown matching script:

Life's A Beach

Saturday July 30th

5:00 PM

The Quinns

444 Bay Avenue

R.S.V.P 609.226.6000

Totally cute! My yard looks great. The pool is sparkling clean. I had sand shipped in and put down by the entrance to the dock. Greye and Field have been collecting shells for me at the beach every Sunday. I put them all over the sand; around the deck they are ashtrays or have little tea lights in them. Up on the table for the food shells hold down the napkins. I bought cheap wind chimes on the boardwalk that have seashells hanging from them. My plates, napkins and toothpicks all have shells on them. My spreading knives have a shell handle. Jeanie is in the kitchen cooking and setting up the bar. Her toothpicks even have a little shell at the top and the staff is wearing all white. "Sloop John B," by the Beach Boys plays on the surround sound outside and in. It is an all white theme. White flowers float in the pool. I could not think of a white signature drink so I decided white wine would do. Jeanie will have it butlered with water as well. All my tables are covered in white tablecloths and we even rented white trays to serve all the food on. White balloons sway in the breeze on our dock. I invited my friends and the shore friends. Kitty never comes to my parties. She also never RSVPs which is so rude! Of course, I haven't heard from her. Mommie always taught me to return all of my calls and RSVP.

"Jeanie, I'm going to go get dressed," I say letting Jeanie know where she can find me.

"Great," Jeanie says without looking up. We are very comfortable together.

I grab a glass of white wine and head up stairs to put on my white silk full-length halter dress from Lilly Pulitzer. It will hide the fact that I'm wearing white flip-flops. I will be standing all night. Husband had to go into the hospital to see a patient. He will be back any minute. I don't stress over entertaining. I love it! Mommie had dinner parties once a month when she and Daddy were still married. She cooked everything from scratch. I have Jeanie so it's even easier. Wine helps. The boys are at Nana's for a sleepover. We have the house to ourselves. As I am putting in my Craig Drake gold flower earrings with diamonds in the center

(I have a matching cocktail ring too) Jeanie calls up, "Your friends are here." *It's 4:50, who the fuck is here!*

"I'll be right down," I call as Husband walks in. Trailing behind him is Kitty. She looks drunk already.

"Kitty!" I exclaim as she sits on my bed and then proceeds to lie back and cross her legs. Husband gently kisses me and then opens his closet to pull out the clothes I picked out. A custom Taglia white linen shirt with Brooks Brothers linen shorts—kahki.

"I'm exhausted. I was out on the beach all day." She is still white as a ghost.

"Where's Kit?" I ask, they really are never in the same room.

"Out on your dock looking at your boat. He wants a new one," Kitty sounds annoyed. She looks over at Husband and slurs, "I love a man in scrubs." She is waiting for Husband to answer her. *Enough of this!*

I put my cocktail ring on and demand, "Kitty come help me light the Tiki torches." I walk out of the room. She eventually follows. Husband may like when women come on to him but he certainly isn't going to return the favor. Not in front of me!

My party is a total hit. Merrits Husband jumped into the pool and is naked. I am shocked Kitty actually showed. Thank God Pippa's in Camden. Everyone is having a blast. "Do you think Kitty was hitting on Husband?" I ask Allegra who is wearing a white dress from a surf shop. She is tan!

"God, I doubt it," Says Allegra.

"Why?" I love Husband.

"Kitty needs a lot more money than Husband," Allegra says matter of factly.

"Oh, yes your right." It was such a strange thing to say.

"Did you meet my new shore friends?" I ask looking around for Sue, Lisa and Denise.

"No." Allegra answers, she's in a bad mood. I should ask why.

Instead I say, "Well you should. They are very nice and might need jewelry."

Allegra smiles, "You'll have to introduce me." She knows I won't. At my parties I stand in one place so everyone, especially Jeannie, can find me. Another PR strategy.

I'm not sure when everyone left. I go to bed at 9:00. Life's a beach was a total success. Of course, none of my Main Line friends talked to any of my shore friends.

Chapter XXI

MALE ATTENTION: A MUST

"It" girls have a gay best friend.

"Kenny?" I say, as he answers his phone.

"Hi, honey," Kenny, says back, "Anna's been asking when you are coming to New York for lunch." Kenny's being silly, "what's going on?"

"What do I wear?" as I stare at my walk-in closet holding my cordless phone, standing in my lace underwear and bra. I always wear lace underwear and bra. Lace is elegant on lingerie, not on clothes. Plus, even if you aren't planning to, you should always be prepared to be seen naked (another rule). I do wear white cotton underwear when I exercise, but that is the only time.

"Where are you going?" Kenny asks.

"Kitty's for an Academy Ball committee meeting," I sigh. Kitty probably has all LA PERLA lingerie.

"Honey, you know you always look fantastic. Wear the JM orange silk pants with the bumble bees on them," Kenny suggests.

"I don't know. I am feeling so uninspired," I say.

"Poodle, I have to go, my boss is calling me, so call me after the meeting and let me know how it went." Kenny clicks off.

Everything I am trying on is either too tight or does not look good. This is sending me into a deep depression and a very bad mood. I must resist or I will have a very bad day at the meeting. Quick! I'll wear an old standby short sleeved black cashmere sweater with black shorts and quilted Chanel ballet flats. Whew! Feeling better already. Must find gold signet earrings and Hermès scarf. Then my outfit will be complete. I throw on a long black cashmere wrap and am officially glamorous and no one will be able to tell I still have a lot of baby weight to lose.

As I drive to Haverford, Mommie calls. "Elizabeth, Bonnie from the Devon Horse Show called, and they would like to put little Field in the opening parade next spring."

"Isn't he too young, Mommie?" I ask.

"No, he will be two, and that is a perfect age, but we must plan his outfit," Mommie trills. "Emily Lacey monogram roll neck sweater perhaps," Mommie adds.

"Not now, Mother, I'm driving. Can I call you tonight?" I say with a little too much irritation in my voice. "Don't leave me this way," by Jimmy Somerville plays on the radio.

"Okay," Mommie kisses as she hangs up the phone. This is what Mommie does when she is not skiing. Although I don't recall Mommie ever on a horse, during the spring and summer she attends all of the Main Line horse events. I suppose this is how one entertains oneself when one does not have children. She and her friends plan over the top tailgates and compete with other people for the blue ribbon, which, of course Mommie's tailgate always wins. The First City Troop's Borderplate kicks the whole Main Line horse season off. Then Radnor Hunt, The Devon Horse Show and lastly, The Dressage at Devon Horse Show. This year she got the blue ribbon for they're ho down theme. They brought a pick up truck and filled it with hay. It was brilliant. Someone played a banjo. The tailgate even had a bar that looked like one from a Western movie. Not that I have ever watched a Western movie. Honestly, they plan these tailgates like weddings. Mommie refused to wear cowboy boots. Mommie prefers St. John.

Now "Life in one day," by Howard Jones plays on the radio.

When I arrive at Kitty's I see her through the window, locked in her laundry room, arguing on the phone. I wonder... *who is she talking to?* Of course, her perfectly clean sparkling Lexus SUV is parked on the driveway with the plate, MLKITTY. *Ugh, gross!*

Mimi greets me at the door with a smile "JM is opening a men's store."

"Really, when?" I say enthusiastically. Mimi always has the best dirt. I try to keep up but I think she's winning.

"It will be next month in Spread Eagle Village. We'll have to go to the opening," Mimi says as she drags me into the living room. Kitty is nowhere to be seen, but the house is perfect as usual. Does she even have children? There isn't a toy in sight. They are probably forced to read and recite poetry like in one of those Jane Austen novels. Life looked pretty boring in that movie "Sense and Sensibility." All they did was read, knit, drink tea and wait for people to stop by and visit. *Dull!* Then Kitty appears.

"Ladies, I want to thank everyone for their help. Let's do a brief recap and then I have lunch for everyone." Kitty is standing at the entrance to her living room. *Has she gained weight,* I wonder? "Elizabeth, how are we on the raffles?"

"Good! Everyone confirmed on the list except for The Plaza," I say with confidence, since I have done nothing for the last month but stalk these people.

"Did you hear back from Frida Giannini?" Kitty asks while staring at me intently.

Who the fuck is Frida Giannini? "Not yet, Kitty, but I'll follow up tomorrow and let you know." Whew, saved by my grace and charm. I'm getting sick of this bullshit!

"But it's not even on your raffle list," Kitty presses.

I have not even heard of this person. My guess is that it's a designer, and she is trying to make me look stupid. *Bitch!* "I'm on it, Kitty, no worries," I say, remaining calm even though I'm turning red and starting to sweat. Too much cashmere!

Finally Kitty moves on to put someone else in front of the firing squad. At least I am done reporting to her as I crack open a Diet Coke and sit back.

Later Kitty finds me. "Elizabeth, who is your trainer again?"

"I still work out with Nicki from the racquet club; why, do you use someone new?" I answer, noticing a society photographer has arrived to shoot the meeting. Why are they always at her house?

"I've been going to Eric, have you ever seen him?" Kitty asks.

"No, he's new?" *Why is she asking me this?*

"Yes, I think he has the hots for me," Kitty smiles, looking like she is on Percocet.

"I'm sure he does," I smile back as I look for a way to get out of the conversation but also not be photographed. I wonder if Eric is better than Nicki? Maybe I'll switch too.

Mimi strides over. "Who wants to go to the trunk show at the cricket club?"

"I'll go. Do they serve wine?" I laugh, as we walk out the door.

That was bizarre. Kitty is so insecure; all she cares about is male attention. I don't think I would like working out with a man. I would be self-consciences they would think my butt is fat. Not Kitty though. She probably flirts with him the whole time. I always notice at parties she only talks to men. Pathetic! Of course, I call Colby to tell her. "Who is Frida Giannini?" I ask, knowing Colby was in fashion.

"The new designer for Gucci," Colby says confidently. Colby can't be on the committee for Academy Ball this year. She was on it last year. And they like to rotate people so everyone can have a turn.

"Oh. I refuse to think of anyone but Tom Ford," I say trying to sound like I know what I'm talking about. "There was a society photographer at the event. Is that strange?" I guess I don't know as much as I thought.

"Sort of. I wonder who invited a society photographer," Colby contemplates. We get off the phone as Mimi and I arrive at Merion Cricket Club.

"So guess what Kitty said to me before you got to the meeting," Mimi is smiling.

"What?" *Oh god now what.*

"I was saying something about Fiancé and she said Mimi remember the key to a good marriage is blow jobs. Even if you don't feel like giving them, do. Just remind yourself that they are good for your facial muscles and sex is good for your serotonin. Serotonin makes your face glow and keeps you skinny!" Mimi imitates her trill.

"Jesus! What is wrong with her?" *That is so gross!*

"She's warped," Mimi laughs. "I get a kick out of her sometimes." *I don't.* Mimi's more laid back than me.

"Before I forget, we have to plan your shower," I say changing the Kitty subject.

"Oh, just call my mother." Mimi could care less about her shower. Mimi thinks showers are queer. She is too cool for school.

I wonder if I blow jobs help you facial muscles stay younger. Sex makes you thin? Who knew? Note to self: *try it.*

SC Secret Services

Tracie Martin Facials (takes 5 years off in one session since we all still want to look 26)

Oxygen Facials from Bliss (helps your arteries if you smoke)

Laura Norman Reflexology (helps with weight loss)

Skylar Moriss Hypnosis (also for losing weight)

Vitamin shots

Injections: Botox and Restalyne

Intense Pulse light therapy

Dermatologists

Teeth bleach

Handwriting class

French Manis and Pedis

Brazilian Bikini Wax

Bikini facial (the only way to deal with the pain of the bikini wax)

Hair highlights

Eyebrow dying and waxing

Eyelash extensions

Eyelash dying

Hot stone massage (helps with detox and stress)

Piano Lessons

Hair extensions

Cornelia Facials

Voice Lessons (One must speak properly)

Hide all of these services from Husbands and Friends!

RayBan

Prada
Sunglasses

Brooks Brothers
Suit

Mink
Coat

Mikimoto
Pearls

Tiffanys

Dior
Bag

Michael Kors

Christian
Louboutins

Belgian
Shoes

8.

Chapter XXII

SEPTEMBER VOGUE

Fall is almost here! I love fall. I look good in fall colors. Plus, this is when "It" all begins. Today I am supposed to be meeting with the committee for Shore Memorial Hospital. Besides being on committees in Philadelphia, because of Husband's job, I am also on four hospital committees. Shore Memorial—doesn't actually need any money, but we always pretend it does, and throw fundraisers for it at various casinos. Atlantic City Medical Center truly needs money, so we have a fundraiser for it at the convention hall where The Miss America pageant was held. I always practice my model walk on the stage during set-up. I am also on the committee for The RNS Ball, which is a cancer and heart disease non-profit. I am making progress on friends at the shore. And lastly, I am on the committee for Wills Eye Hospitals "Eye Ball." Since the city owns the hospital, we all suspect there is something fishy going on, but of course we never say anything. So you can see I am extremely busy, but as soon as I get the mail and realize that The September *Vogue* has arrived, which I have read religiously since I was 13, I cancel all my appointments for the day and retire to my bedroom, extremely excited.

In the fall I always change purses too (more rules). Allegra switches purses daily. In all 30 of her bags she has: gum, lighter, sunglasses, lipstick, and a pen. She only has to grab her wallet, keys and cell phone. I can't be bothered with all that. I carry either a brown Louis or a beige Chanel. Then in the winter I switch to a black JM bag and in the spring a candy apple green Kate Spade. In the summer I have a dozen Bermuda bags, a Coach basket weave bag, and cloth bags from Molly B. Just as I am settling into bed the phone rings. I crane my neck, leaning to see who is calling on the caller ID. It's Kitty. *What!?* She knows I have a committee meeting today. What does she want, more raffle updates?

"Hello," I say trying to sound sick so as to stick with my alibi.

"Nana," Kitty asks in her high-pitched trill.

"No, Kitty, it's Elizabeth, I'm home sick, what's up?" I say, praying this won't take too long.

"Elizabeth," Kitty sounds ever so slightly shaken. "Oh, I was just calling to say thank you for everything you are doing and say that Kit and I want to have you for dinner soon. Uh, I was calling figuring I would get your voice mail," Kitty stutters and is overcompensating. *What is going on?*

"Thanks, Kitty. Look, I really don't feel well. Can I call you tomorrow?" I ask, still trying to figure out what is going on.

"Sure, sure," Kitty hangs up. *What was that?* Was she calling for Nana? I overheard her saying to someone that she is having staffing issues with the girls (a.k.a brats). Is she trying to steal my nanny? I'll kill her!

When Husband arrives home later that evening, he calls, "Hi, honey, how are you?"

"I am sick. I was in bed all day," I say listlessly, trying to look tired and pathetic, even though I'm wearing ivory silk pajamas with ivory cashmere slippers from Nimis, which garners sympathy from Husband.

"I'm sorry, Elizabeth. What can I do for you?"

"Will you get me a glass of wine?" I ask as I pass by to the living room, where Field and Greye are watching cartoon network.

"Hi, Mommie," Greye says without glancing away from the TV. Field crawls into my lap to snuggle.

"Hi, Greye, who's the love of Mommie's life?" I ask, as this is one of our things. I will teach Field when he is old enough to really talk.

"Me!" Replies Greye in his sweetest E.T. alien sounding voice.

"And who made you so cute?" I continue.

"Mommie," Greye says on cue. Sometimes when he is being funny he will say Daddy, but he knows I made him gorgeous. I must admit, I make beautiful babies, I think as I sit back with a glass of Sterling Chardonnay, my favorite of the month. Field opens his mouth and gurgles something and then gives me a huge smile. I feel warm and content as I begin to ponder what to wear tomorrow. I like Chardonnay from California only, and I don't like it to be too expensive. I also must drink it out of a wine glass from Williams Sonoma, Riedel. If the glass is too thick, or god forbid plastic, the flavor just isn't the same. The wine must have been chilled in the freezer for an hour so it is very, very chilly! Of course, if it is served to me incorrectly, I never say a word as it would appear too snobby. I never want people to think I am a princess, except if they actually mistook me as a princess. That would be très flattering!

My personal chef service, Jeannie, calls. We all use the same chef service too. It's very incestuous. We all use the same cleaning lady (Joan), trainer (Nicki), masseuse (Cindy), chef (Jeannie), and nutritionist (Helen). You name it. It's strange, and I can't quite understand it, but I guess my theory would be we give each other recommendations. Also, it's like you don't want anyone to be getting something better than you. I haven't had time to really figure out this phenomenon. Probably no one wants to be left out. I always get chicken two nights and then seafood the rest of the week because Colby's father says fish will help me stay young looking. I don't feel young, though. I feel tired some days. I don't know how I can go on at this pace for another 40 years. I can't think about that now, because if I do, I might have a nervous breakdown. I hope I don't live past 80. Holly Golightly called it the "mean reds" in the movie Breakfast at Tiffany's. I think red is too bright of color to describe how I feel when I am loathing myself or worrying about life. I have a fear of being alone and being ugly. I have other, more real fears: being paralyzed, being raped, having chronic pain, and my children being abducted, molested or dying. I wonder if it's normal that I worry about my children dying all the time.

Allegra and I are meeting at the Union League for a drink to discuss her latest love quest, or rather, love failure. I read an article once that said that people experience the same pain from a breakup that they do if they are stabbed. In other words, your brain processes pain from a breakup and pain from being physically wounded in the same area (right lobe). It makes perfect sense because rejection is the worst feeling in the entire world. It is always that age-old question with Allegra, "Why didn't he call?" "Why doesn't he like me?"

"That's why it hurts so badly, because your brain just can't stand rejection. It's like being completely beat up," I say with sympathy.

After our long conversation, Allegra decides, "I deserve better." Then we get onto important matters.

"What time shall I make our appointments at Elizabeth Arden Red Door?" I ask.

"The usual time," Allegra says starting to smile. I knew this would make her feel better. We secretly go to The Red Door the first Saturday of every month. It is in Absecon, New Jersey and absolutely no one knows about it, which makes it the perfect escape. We meet at 2:00 PM for a steam and sauna. Then we get waxed, massaged and top it off with facials. We always stop off after for a glass of wine. It is our little secret, because we don't want others tagging along and ruining our fun. In the summer we can use their pool and in the winter we use the Jacuzzi. Day spas are nice but Red Door in Absecon, NJ is like going to The Greenhouse, but we don't have to fly to Dallas.

I read an article once in the *New York Times* magazine, (my favorite. It comes on Sunday with the Style section) that said that people aren't good forecasters of their future and their future happiness. They can't predict what will make them happy. They think that they want something, and when they get it, it will make them happy forever. The problem is that it is like raising the bar. When you get it that thing that you thought will make you happy for eternity, you get used to it, and it doesn't make you happy anymore.

As you can see, I read a lot. It's a great way to learn new information. Books by Edith Wharton are amazing, good reads and great to study. Obviously, the best magazines are *Vanity Fair, W, Vogue* and *Town & Country. Vanity Fair* is the hardest to read. If you can read *Vanity Fair*, which means that you are way smart. Next to the *New York Times* Style section, *Town & Country* is the definite bible. *Town & Country* is where I learned about Miss Trish of Capri. How else would I have found out about those cute shoes? If you are from the Philadelphia Main Line, you really don't get to the Hamptons that often. We have other options, but reading publications like *Town and Country* teaches you important fashion items located in other States.

"Its just that I have had so many dates I can't even remember their names anymore," Allegra says going back to the subject.

"Allegra, don't worry. You'll meet the right guy. Its just going to take a while because you are an AT and guys are threatened," I say supportively. I have a theory that men need to marry below them. A man needs to feel like *the* man, and if he is with a princess like Allegra he will feel like a loser. I mean, she is so "It." Men want to be the strong guy that knows everyone and has all the connections. Males are insecure babies with inferiority complexes. That is why most SCs deep down don't like their husbands. My husband is secure and smart so we don't have to play those reindeer games.

It dawns on me that Allegra and my life are starting to sound like an Olsen Twin movie. Secretly, Allegra and I love the Olsen Twin movies; another guilty pleasure. Anything with Lindsey Lohan, or Hillary Duff is the definite best movie ever. You can watch all of those depressingly sad movies like "Million Dollar Baby" and try to feel deep, yet, at the end of the day, if you want to feel good, watch Lizzy McGuire or New York Minute, and you'll feel better. I know that sounds painfully shallow. They say laughter is the best medicine. Light, senseless movies always keep my mind off things when I feel down. It is just like I was saying earlier, I want the world to be a beautiful place, and fun movies like Freaky Friday are so lovely they make the world a better place. We don't even read books that are geared for our demographic. We like tween books. "You know what you need," I say knowingly.

"What?" Allegra asks depressed.

"Gossip Girl. They're funny books and it will totally remind you of college and keep your mind off all of this guy stuff," I say as I write down the title.

SOCIAL CLIMBERS CINEMA:

Metropolitan

Annie

Breakfast Club

Mean Girls

Royal Tanenbaums

The Philadelphia Story

Bringing up Baby

Maid to Order

Pretty in Pink

House of Yes (Anything with Parker Posey. Best in Show et al)

Clueless

How To Steel A Million

The Talented Mr. Ripley

Heathers

Overboard

Baby Boom

My Fair Lady

Malice

Can't Buy Me Love

Barcelona

Last Days of Disco

It Girls

Born Rich

Jagged Edge

Everyone Says' I Love You

Confessions of a Teenage Drama Queen

Legally Blonde

Working Girl

Van Wilder

Hitch

Sabrina

Scotland, Pennsylvania

First Wives Club

Sixteen Candles

The Titanic

Sweet Home Alabama

Cruel Intentions

The Age of Innocence

The Fab Five—The Texas Cheerleading Scandal

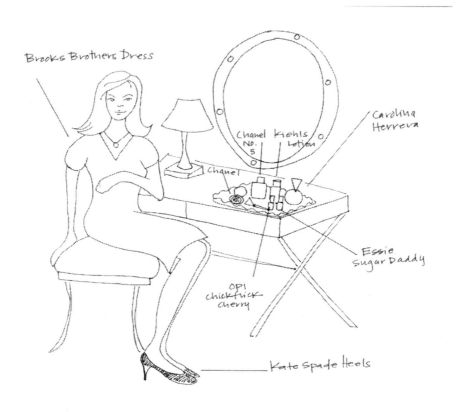

Brooks Brothers Dress

Carolina Herrera

Chanel No. 5

Kiehls Lotion

Chanel

Essie Sugar Daddy

OPI Chickflick Cherry

Kate Spade Heels

Chapter XXIII

How To Spend Your Day

"It" girls belong to the right clubs and lunch there. Over lunch at The Racquet Club, Allegra and I are discussing the latest committee we are on, and dieting. Dieting is another huge topic. Why can't we lose weight? Why we need to lose another five pounds. I read another article once that said people aren't good at self-control when faced with a situation that would challenge it. They usually go against their goal to be in control. In other words, I could have said to myself this morning that I am going to eat really healthy all day. Then, when all of a sudden at lunch, you are faced with Crème Brulée, you can't remember why in the morning you were so fixated on being a healthy eater. That's because when people are faced with options, they feel like they want to take them and live their lives to the fullest! Life should be fun and, people do not like to be held back. They can't focus on something in the long term. That is why people do stupid things and, in the end, regret it. We can't picture the future and want the immediate gratification. Behaving is hard work!

Allegra is on the Sonoma diet. She does not need to be on a diet, but this one allows wine. I am doing the South Beach diet. We would never do Weight Watchers; too bourgeois. Dieting is a huge obsession. There is a ranking system to obsessions. Rank: #1: What to wear. #2: Dieting. #3: Committees. #4: Everything else. My entire life is one big obsession.

Allegra and I also review all the invitations we receive and decide which events are worth attending. It dawns on me that I have not been following up on picking up any raffles for Academy Ball. *Shit!* "I better work really hard on this committee or people are going to get very mad at me. I need to start calling these people so I actually get the goods."

"Don't worry, Elizabeth. Who will actually be mad at you? Kitty the UB?" Allegra says.

"I hate to be shallow, but I just received Pippa's gift for Field," I say feeling guilty for being a gossip and possibly being rude.

"What did she give you?" asks Allegra.

"Well, besides the fact that it is a year overdue, they are pajamas are from Children's Place," I say carefully waiting for Allegra's reaction.

"What? That is so gross. It's like a chain, right?" Allegra is being her terrific opinionated self.

"Yes, and quite frankly, Pippa should know I only put the boys in Petit Badeau until they are two." I am still trying to be careful. Allegra, occasionally, gets on her high horse and acts so self-righteous, as if she never looks down on people. It is so annoying when she is in one of those moods. I hate being lectured. I also despise being patronized.

"You can take the girl out of the ghetto, but you can't take the ghetto out of the girl. She will always be NR," Allegra says assuredly.

Bingo! She gets it. I mean, who would buy clothes from that store? I know Pippa was trying to be nice, but get a grip! When your last name is Pew, you have to give a certain level of gift, and Children's Place is not it.

Just then, I see Kitty walk by. I grab Allegra's arm and do the whole wide-eyed "shhh! so she won't see us" face. She is heading right to the locker room, probably to meet with her new personal trainer. Nicki did finally tell me that Kitty moved on to the new guy. Even thought I knew I didn't say a word. But what Kitty didn't mention, and Nicki did, is apparently Kitty helped get Eric the job. *Weird.*

Allegra starts talking again, but I am not even listening. I am thinking about Kitty's outfit. Clothing completely distracts me. It is really cute. *I wonder where she got it. I wonder who the designer is. Maybe Millie? I love that designer, too cute.* I love clothing. I'm a total girl; I was not a tomboy. I preferred Barbie's.

"Uh, I am going into the locker room," I say interrupting Allegra.

"Why?" Allegra says somewhat annoyed. I cut her off.

"I'll be right back," I say as I get up to spy on Kitty. She has already left the locker room, and her clothes are in a pile on the floor. *How cheap can you be to not rent a locker? Whatever.* This is better for me so I can look through her bag. Just as I suspected, her clothes are by a beautiful designer Narcisso Rodriguez. *Note to self: I must go to Bergdorfs,* I decide as I run out of the locker room. Instead I say, "Bathroom," I smile as I sit back down at the table as Allegra frowns at me. I can't tell her what I did, or I will look like a stalker.

When I get home my family is in the hot tub, Husband and my two monkeys. They are all yelling, "Mommie, watch me!" It is the cutest thing in the whole world. Everyone should have dozens of children, especially if they are boys. Males are so much more fun to watch because they are more active. Having sons is most prestigious. Men always want their family name carried on. I am thrilled to have two sons. I have a glass of Chardonnay and a cigarette, and sit and talk to my family for the rest of the night. "Apache," by The Sugar Hill Gang plays on my iPhone.

SOCIAL CLIMBER SHOWS:

Nip Tuck

Weeds

Dirt

The Real Housewives of New York City

Santa Barbara

Girls Next Door

Falcon Crest

Desperate Housewives

Filthy Rich Cattle Drive

The Jeffersons'

The Simple Life

Dallas

Gastineau Girls

Dynasty

How To Be A Hilton

Different Strokes

90210

Arrested Development

The OC

The Apprentice

Melrose Place

Dirty Sexy Money

Any Soap Opera, Especially "One Life to Live" as the writer is from The Main Line

Chapter XXIV

How To Entertain At Home

Every year Kit and Kitty have an annual Halloween party. They invite all their old friends from High School. This is my least favorite holiday ever. I don't like to look ugly. So the only thing I can dress as is a witch, where I can wear a black cocktail dress, a witch hat, and lots of gold jewelry. If I were a witch that is how I would dress. Or I can be a tennis player. The cute white skirts show off my legs. One year I tried to be a skier but that was a disaster. I tripped Bryn with on of my ski poles. Plus it was hot with the parka. I've decided to be a witch but in Ernest Jeans, this is completely unlike me. I never wear jeans. I wear them with super high silver leopard print Manolo Blahnik's—Sedaraby style. And a plain black t-shirt from Club Monaco. I wonder who is going to be there that I haven't seen in forever. I dress Husband as a preppy. He let's me pick out his clothes for parties, not work. Husband is colorblind. You should see what he puts together and walks out of this house in! It doesn't bother me if he wants to look like a fool. I certainly don't want all the nurses at the shore after Husband. By the way that totally happens. I know a doctor's wife who caught him in their bed with a nurse. Now she has new breast implants and a monstrous diamond ring. But anyway, I dress Husband well for parties. I have him in head to toe madras, with a sweater tied around his neck. Penny loafers for his feet, with penny's in them. The collar up on his shirt. Husband looks ridiculous. Very funny!

As we arrive I spot Colby standing with a drink, smoke is coming out of it. "Hello!" I wave as we kiss. "What is that?" I ask.

"I don't know but it's potent. Kitty is using these goblets that look like skeleton heads." Colby adds impressed with Kitty's entertaining abilities. *I'm not drinking that*--it might be grain alcohol. And we all remember what happens when I drink grain shots.

As I am ordering a glass of wine I see someone out of the corner of my eye. *Shit!* It's Duncan. Duncan has been living in Chicago. When we were in college his father opened one of their Wilson Paint stores there. Wilson Paints is like a Sherwin Williams except it only exists where the Wilson's live or vacation. So unless you have been to Lake Forest, The Main Line or Palm Beach you won't see one. God I really screwed up Kitty's SS by sleeping with Duncan. Thank god she found Kit or she would ostracize me the way she ostracizes Pippa. I would literally be invited to nothing. I turn my back to him so I can get some Chardonnay Pshychology. "I like your outfit," I say to Colby willing her to talk to me and keep me occupied so Duncan does not come over. We have to look really serious. I will try to inch us away from the bar. That is where everyone hangs out and with the amount Duncan drinks; he will be there shortly. Colby is dressed as a doctor, she does this every year. Since her husband and father are both doctors she has lots of scrubs to choose from. She looks really cute.

"Thanks, I'm original aren't I?" She says as I signal to move to get out of the way. Secretly wanting to flee the party. If Kitty sees us talk she will explode.

Later as I exit the bathroom Duncan is standing right there. "Hi," I say with a warm smile as he embraces me and won't let go. "Fallen Angel," by Alphaville is blaring from the living room.

"You look more beautiful now than you did when we were younger," Duncan says softly into my ear finally letting me go, a little. "You have the prettiest face I have every seen in person." *As opposed to what? A movie star?*

I pull back further but he still has his hands on my arms. I have major butterflies. I hope I don't blush. "Thank you. What are you doing in town?" I ask, keep it light.

"My Parents anniversary party is tomorrow," Duncan says while staring deeply into my eyes. He is trashed. I hope Husband does not see us. Not that he knows we slept together.

"Congratulations. That is wonderful. It is so nice to see you," I have to end this and go.

"You two Elizabeth, you know I always had such a crush on you in high school," *Jesus!* Duncan smiles.

"You're funny. I love you too. Not to cut you off but I have to locate Husband so we can get home." I say turning in a mock "look for him" way. And there she is. *Fuck*! Kitty saw the whole thing. Like a zombie on Percocet she is standing at the bottom of her staircase watching us talk.

Kitty continues to stare. And then I see the glare.

Duncan sees the look on my face and turns to look at her, finally releasing his hands from mine. "Hi, Kitty!" Duncan slightly slurs.

Kitty's face changes instantly. Now she is trying to look seductive. *Gross.* Kitty licks her lips and pushes them out into a pout.

Duncan starts to walk towards her. He falters ever so slightly and then stands up tall and walks to give her a hug. Which I notice, he lets go of right away.

Passing by the two, wanting to puke, I say "Kitty this is the best Halloween party yet. Thank you so much for having us."

"You're Welcome," Kitty says lightly to me. "I am so glad you're in town Duncan," is the last thing I hear Kitty say to Duncan as I make it to the other room.

That was awkward. I try to locate Colby. "Colby," I yell across the living room. Colby waves me over. She is talking to Bryn. I can't tell her in front of Bryn.

Pacing through the house. *I have to go! Where is Husband?* I locate Husband in Kit's office; they are looking at a sailing chart or something. *Cute.* "Husband, we should get going to relieve Nana," I don't want to sound like I am not having a good time.

"I am so glad you guys made the trip," Kit says shaking Husband's hand and I give a thank you kiss on the cheek. Kit smiles. Kit and Husband sail together occasionally at the yacht club. Kit grew up sailing at Camp Pasquaney on Newfound Lake in New Hampshire. It is the oldest camp in the United States. Established in 1985, very elite. I want to send the boys there.

"We'll see you at the next event," I say dying to get out of there.

Kit just rolls his eyes, "Yeah, see you soon." Now he is shaking his head a little.

Walking out to the car we pass by the kitchen where the door is wide open. It must be hot in there. I hear Kitty screaming on the top of her lungs at the staff "You are not stocking the bar fast enough. People have to wait for drinks!" She continues her tirade as Husband and I just stare at one another. What a UB. "And wipe down the fucking counter, what if someone saw it like that! I am so pisssed!" Kitty snaps.

Safely in the car, I can't believe Kitty would talk to people like that. ATs are especially nice to staff and help. Only SCs talk down to people.

I decide to myself to tell no one about what Duncan said to me. I need this situation to die. *Is this going to hang over my head for the rest of my life?*

"In your eye's," by Peter Gabrielle is on the CD. *NEXT song!* I hit skip. That's the fucking song that Duncan and I had playing on that dreadful night. I need to throw out this disk. This situation has to disappear. "Forever live and die," by OMD starts. I need a distraction. I can't think about Duncan and Kitty anymore.

Chapter XXV

Subtle Snubbing

A week later and I am going to my Tea Club again. It is getting colder and colder now that it is almost winter. I am wearing the latest full leg trousers with quilted Delman shoes and a cute little Bouclé blazer (from Escada, don't get excited it's from the outlet store). I love my tea club, but sometimes it is just stressful watching what you drink, what you say and how you act. Then you worry about it later! It can be so daunting. Everyone has little Judith Lieber handbags that hang from their wrists. Of course, they match their outfits and their Judith Lieber sunglasses perfectly. The Tea Club is a tough group. The UB, Kitty Kimmel, is there. She is lucky that her family in law owns Barneys. She has the best style, not nearly as traditional and preppie as the rest of us. (But don't forget I knew her when she was younger, fatter and not as well dressed.)

Anyway, she is talking about the Academy Ball. "The committee is stressful! I am soooo busy right now I don't have a minute to breathe. I never knew it could be so much work," Kitty complains to an audience.

Meanwhile, I haven't seen her do anything. We do all of the work and she sits around, asking what we are doing and getting all of the credit. Plus everyone knows it's charity work, not real work. I'm starting to agree with Allegra, this is all bull shit. I just had an acid glycolic peel so my skin is really refreshed and feeling bright and perky. So even though she is complaining, it's not aging me. Again, she has nothing to complain about. Her life is perfect! She has the latest Lexus and three nannies for her four daughters. (I bet she was trying for a boy.) It is so unfair! The whole deal with an SC is that the whole time we are talking, the conversation keeps reverting back to her. It is just unbelievable how selfish and self-centered one person can be. Can you say narcissist? Then, of course, the society photographers are always snapping this girl's picture. Naturally, she can't wait to be in the pictures and see herself in the paper. She's always in the newspaper. It's nauseating. Don't they want to have diversity? Oh, and this whole time I'm getting the sense that she is jabbing me with negative comments, even though she is trying to be nice to my face. It is like she is undermining me in the conversation the entire time. "Did you see the cover of *Vogue*?" Kitty asks, turning towards me.

"Yes, of course. I love the dress," I say, trying to be polite and interested.

"Well, they ruined it for me. I was going to wear that to Academy Ball, but now I can't," Kitty complains. *Of course she was.* "I'll have to go look for something else. That always happens to me." *Poor Kitty, NOT!*

"When you pick your next dress you should make sure they register it, that way no one can buy it for the same event," I say, trying to act like Kitty has real problems.

"That's a great idea!" Kitty beams.

Why didn't she know about that? "Well, at least you know you have impeccable taste," I say instead with a smile on my face.

"You are funny, Elizabeth. You totally remind me of Pippa right now by the way you are acting," Kitty laughs.

WHAT? She hates Pippa. Because of all that "breaking up the marriage" thing. Kitty is very judgmental. That comment was on purpose! She insulted me to my face! I walk away with this completely icky feeling, dreading the whole thing, and can't wait to find someone else to talk to. I read an article that said the thing you hate most in others is usually a characteristic you yourself possess and loathe. Hmmm. Let's not forget birds of a feather flock together, and maybe she hates Pippa because they are playing the same game, marrying up. After my nauseating conversation with the UB, I bump into Colby. Thank God! She has something fun to talk about because her father just told her about the latest new facial cream.

"LaTherapie," Colby says with her radiant smile. "It's from Paris, and you can only get it in Europe. But," Colby adds "I have the web site where you can order it."

"Why is it so great?" I ask, truly happy to be talking about superficial, extremely important topics such as face care.

"It goes down five layers as opposed to three. Most facial creams in the States only go down three layers," Colby says with confidence.

"Then I must get it. Is it expensive?" I ask.

Colby smiles. She also is telling me cute stories about Sir Lancelot, her teacup bulldog. "I am taking Sir Lancelot to Dressage at Devon. What do you think he should wear?" Colby asks.

"Doesn't he have Burberry?" I wonder what Mommie's tailgate theme will be.

"Yes, but then he would match Kitty's lab." It is unbelievable! We are talking about Kitty Kimmel again. Everything reverts back to her, and everyone is so in love with her (well not my friends). But even if my friends don't like Kitty they will never want to stir the pot. Only Allegra has the guts to zing her. The others want to be on her committees too. Why do people thinks she is so great, and I just can't stand her! However, I must kiss up to her because everyone kisses her ass and thinks that she is so fantastic. She is evil! Thank God my cell phone rings. It's Allegra. She is deeply agonized, as usual, over nothing.

"I must go to Greece for some family thing, and you know I will only fly Swiss Air," Allegra says. She has to have a first class seat for herself and the one next to her. She refuses to sit next to anyone for fear that they might throw up. She's got a big thing with throw up. My theory is Allegra has a stress disorder, she enjoys it.

"I know," I say supportively, thinking could anyone be more high maintenance?

"So anyway, Swiss Air refuses to sell me two seats next to one another because I cannot give them a name. That is so unfair. What am I going to do?" Allegra whines. I am barely listening now.

"Can't you pretend your brother will be flying with you and use his name? Or Frannie, why not Frannie?" Meanwhile, I'm miserable. I'm usually a fun-loving person, but this tea is just way too stuffy. I just have to get out of there.

"Maybe that will work,"Allegra thinks.

"We'll get together this week," I say needing to end the conversation. I am in a bad mood.

As I leave, Kitty shouts, " Love you honey!" *I can't believe this.*

She is so fake. Instead I shout, "Love you, too!" I've got to get better about this because it is starting to show that I absolutely think that she is wretched and that is a bad place to be, not in her good graces. I hate being fake. I am not that talented at it. I'll chalk this up to practicing.

Since Husband is skiing in Stratton, I decide to go to Jacques Ferber Furrier with Allegra. We always need a good dose of shopping. When Husband leaves me, I get upset, lonely and very sad. Husband too misses me a lot. It is an opportunity to buy myself something lavish, and he won't mind as he feels badly he is away. Nothing like a fur coat as a gift. I have three furs. One has my initials in hot pink on the inside, the second has a red monogram and, then for third, I went with the classic tone on tone. I like the shocking colors on the first two. It is so unconventional. They are all minks.

While shopping, Allegra is whispering to me about the night before when she went to visit an ex, Frank, who called her at the last minute to please help him pack for a trip. She didn't want to, but, after much persuading, she went over there to find him in bed, naked, waiting for her. She was so aggravated since she has started a new relationship with

175

a new guy and she wants it to work (Henry). Men can really mess up your life. That's what I am telling her as we overhear somebody in the next room trying on furs who says, "I want this coat to make me look like I'm rich; does it?" We can't believe our ears. We peaked around the corner and there she is, Kitty Kimmel. She is buying a sheared rabbit, but she wants to pass it off as a sheared mink. I can't believe it. She really has to try to look wealthy, *Who does that?!* This is something I will be able to hold over her forever. The thing about Kitty Kimmel is that she seems like a really nice person, but she is trying too hard to be cute. For example, she ends everything in an "ie." For example, call me later on my "cellie" so we can go get "lunchie." It is sort of aggravating when people talk like that—we aren't six.

"Hi, Kitty," I say smiling. "That coat is gorgeous," I say, feeling superior.

"Elizabeth, I had no idea you were here. Hi, Allegra." Kitty looks at us in shock. Like we caught her stealing.

"Christmas gift?" I ask. *Why do I let this girl off the hook all the time?*

"Sort of." Kitty is shifting. "I'll have this picked up tomorrow or you could deliver it, okay?" Kitty asks the sales person. "It" girls know how to get people to do things for them and never have to run their own errands. Note to self: *Delegate.* "Must run ladies. Good to see you, Allegra. Elizabeth, call me later on my cellie." Kitty turns to leave.

"Bye, Kitty," we call after her as Allegra and I smile at each other. "I think her ring looks fake, N.O.C.D." Allegra adds. I wonder if she is onto something.

Later over drinks at George's, Allegra tells me how Frank was waiting in bed for her. She walks in and tries to explain to him that she was going to leave if he wasn't really going to have her help him pack. She said that she wasn't there for sex, and Frank replied, "Oh, come on, Allegra, please. Just this once." She said absolutely not. Then Frank said, " okay, let me just take care of myself." She said absolutely not, I want no part of this. Then he proceeded to masturbate right in front of her, which is totally disgusting.

My advice to Allegra is "Do not worry about it and tell no one." It's just like the time Allegra slept with a married man and then his pregnant wife started calling her on her cell phone and left her threatening voice mails. She said, "I'm pregnant. I heard you had sex with my husband. He has herpes." It was awful. Allegra didn't drink for a whole month she was so upset. What a waste. Men can be really bad and cause all kinds of screw-ups in your life. You're just better off marrying a 1/3 nerd and be done with it.

This is what I am telling Allegra when Mimi and Colby join us. "Hello, Ladies," Mimi says as she flags down the waiter. Mimi is interesting. She consistently has on good khakis and a custom-made white collared shirt, but then a bright pink and green bag with matching shoes and needlepoint belt. So cute! Mimi is a little bit easy. It's a good thing she is getting married. She went to Episcopal the first year it went co-ed. It used to be all boys. She was one of three girls in her class. My theory is that when you are the only girl at a school full of boys going through puberty you get hit on all the time, which increases your chances of male interaction. At an all girls school you don't have as many opportunities with boys, so it is easier to be virtuous. Mimi says it's a good thing she wasn't more attractive, as she has slept with pretty much every guy she has dated. Her theory is, if she had been prettier, her number would be slightly in the high end. She's funny! "I will have a Grey Goose Martini, extra dirty, and she will have a Chardonnay," Mimi says in her matter-of-fact way. There is nothing lady-like about Mimi.

I am sort of sluttish, but in a prudish way. When I say sluttish, I mean I like anyone who is nice to me or compliments me. My favorite compliment is that I look thin. My second is that I look pretty. Telling someone she looks pretty is easy and may not be genuine, so I have to be leery. I am pretty easy. If you say something nice to me I will love you for life. Just don't tell me I'm photogenic, okay. Mimi is a great person and great friend, and tons of fun at parties. She always drinks dirty martinis. We love Mimi.

"So what's new in the land of SCs?" Mimi asks, sipping her drink. Mimi's father is a famous politician; you need to befriend all types of people to get a good range of information. First he was the District Attorney of Philadelphia. Now he is a congressman. There are rumors of an ambassadorship in the future. Mimi and Pippa are best friends. But they pretend they are not and talk behind each other's backs. It gets on Colby's and my nerves, because we get an earful from Mimi about Pippa. "Oh, we haven't spoken all month," Mimi will say and then the next day, we find out they had breakfast together and went to play golf. What? Pippa does the same thing. She will tell us they are not that close, but then next night you will call her and Mimi will be over. Um, hello?

"Not much," Allegra purrs. "How is Pippa?" Allegra asks. Allegra sells a lot of Jewelry to the Pews. Pippa's family in law is very prestigious and don't think she doesn't know it. But she married in—big difference. Can you say way to go SC?

"I don't know," answers Mimi. "What is that smell?" Mimi turns to Colby, who is downing her chardonnay.

"When do you think Pippa will get pregnant?" Colby asks.

"I'm not sure, we haven't discussed it." Mimi says with a knowing look. "But I definitely think it will help things. If you know what I mean." Mimi sips her drink.

"With her husband?" I ask worried.

"No, with the Pews," Mimi clarifies. Mimi has *all* the dirt.

"Pippa's husband is barely speaking to his sister right now. Pippa has caused a lot of tension there." Mimi lights a cigarette and sits back.

"Babies are a beautiful thing," I miss my darlings. "I am much closer with Husbands family now that we have children." It's true. I didn't have a lot in common with them at first. I was the "city" girl. They had never met a debutante before.

"Mimi, what do you do all day?" asks Allegra. Mimi does not work. She doesn't even have children yet. Mimi wanted to be a teacher but when she found out she would have to grade all there homework she decided it was too much aggravation. I think she even looked into hiring an assistant to help her. Mimi shops with her mother all day and does charity work. Mimi's a ditz! In a good way.

"I don't know Allegra," Mimi pauses and sips her martini. "But it takes me all day to do it," Mimi smiles. She is so relaxed in her own skin. I envy that.

Everything is going well at Georges' then Colby's teacup bulldog, Sir Lancelot, is becoming restless in her handbag. So we have to go before we get found out. I think the smell is poop.

Leaving George's is fine because Husband is coming home that night, and I really miss him and want to see him. I am going home to make everything perfect. I listen to "Girlfriend," by Avril Lavigne on the way home.

At home later I am debating how to freshen up. I have this secret of wearing Crabtree and Evelyn's spring rain lotion and Carolina Herrera perfume, the original, of course. They smell really nice together. I even put Crabtree and Evelyn's spring rain soaps in all of my drawers and spray all of my Mason Pierson hair brushes with Carolina Herrera perfume, so I smell amazing all the time. I spray spring rain room spray over my bed every morning. Men can be smelly when they sleep. I like to have light floral scents in my upstairs, so I have spring- scented potpourri and candles that I refresh each summer upstairs. Then down stairs I like everything to smell like cinnamon. It blends better with the smell of cooking and my coffee in the morning. So every fall I put out tons of apple cinnamon potpourri and candles. I change into toile pants and a black cashmere turtleneck, brush my hair with my Mason Pearson hairbrush, from England, to give it new body. I also hope it hides the smell of smoke. I like to look nice always anyway. Maybe we'll go out for dinner. I sit down with a glass of wine looking through *Vogue*, hoping to decide what I'd buy for winter. If the waspy/preppy look is so out, then why is Ralph Lauren so popular? I love the lady-like look. I am very traditional no matter what's in *Vogue*. I love looking at magazines to get ideas. My phone rings. It is Allegra. Allegra is so funny. She even has a ship named after her (obviously it is so "It" to have a ship named after you), "The ANGELLI ALLEGRA." Anyway, she is totally freaking out because she always wears the same red nail polish by OPI- Chick Flick Cherry on her toes.

"Frannie is wearing Chick Flick Cherry," is all she says. Fran is Allegra's slave. She tells people Frannie was her nanny when she was little but I would say now that Allegra is 33, Frannie is her full time maid.

"I like that color." I don't feel like getting into it with her right now. Enough drama for one day.

"Well, I swear that I am never going to wear it again!" Allegra hangs up.

Husband always says my friends are crazy. Allegra and Colby have absolutely zero problems. Well, that isn't true. Colby does have one problem. Her nannies are always quitting on her or leaving in the middle of the night. She must not be very nice to them because they always quit. Colby is always complaining endlessly about her nanny problems. Really, how hard can she have it? She gets to take a nap every afternoon. I never get to take a nap. Anyway, Allegra complaining about her red nail polish and about her maid stealing her idea reminds me of when she was little. Her grandmother told me this story. She would go up to groups of people and say, "Hi, lets play King and Queen. I'll be the Queen, and you are all going to be my slaves." In Greek, of course.

The other thing Allegra always reminds me: "you people think you are so cool for being off the Mayflower? Well you were all losers in Europe and had to come over here on a boat to get away and start over. I flew here first class." Well, she does have a point.

Then in walks Husband and my two sons. I can't wait to hear their little voices. They sound like little extraterrestrials, the way they speak. "Mommie, Mommie!" And "I love you!" Field and Greye are the cutest things in the entire world. It almost hurts when I hear them. I love it so much. It is like a wound that will always be on my heart and never heal when I hear my little boys talk about the things that interest them. Heath Ledger was quoted as saying "Having a child is like having a lump in your throat forever." I couldn't agree more.

"We missed you," Husband says as he hands me a little bag with tissue. Husband brilliantly picked up cashmere sweatpants for me at TSE. I am feeling warm and happy all over.

"Thank you! I love them. Welcome home!" I exclaim as I envelop the boys in a group hug. Husband gently kisses me on the cheek, "How was the skiing? I want every detail," I ask, so excited they are home. I snuggle my boys onto the couch to hear all about the Stratton trails.

SOCIAL CLIMBER'S MAGAZINES:

Town and Country

Vogue

NY Times Style Magazine

Q

New York Magazine

W

Bazaar

Hampton Magazine

Ocean Drive

BUCKS $$

Vanity Fair

Robb Report

Architectural Digest

The New York Post

Philadelphia Style

Gulfshore Life

House and Garden

People

Forbes 400

Main Line Magazine

Veranda

Naples

Quintessential Style

Fortune 500

Beth Dunn

Us Weekly

New Jersey Life

Surface

Quest

Vive

OK!

Elle

Philadelphia Magazine

Saving and rereading Charity Ball Program Books

Chapter XXVI

TRAVEL

"It" girls travel. A lot. As I run to answer the phone, I bump into the couch. That will totally leave a mark! (I hate having any blemishes on my flawless complexion, particularly the skin on my face), I think as I answer "Hello," I say clueless because I did not have time to check the caller id.

"Elizabeth, it's Allegra," Allegra sounds confused, wondering why I didn't know it was her.

"Hi, sorry, I was running for the phone. What's up? How was Aspen?" I ask eagerly. How I wish I could have gone. I loved the year we lived there.

"Good." Allegra takes these kinds of trips with a grain of salt. Nothing impresses her.

"What is everyone wearing?" I need to know the trends, in case I am behind.

"You know, the usual parkas and pants, and a fur every now and then," Allegra says in her Greek accent sounding bored at my bourgeois attempt to keep up.

"That's distressing. All I have are suits. Should I buy separates for Stratton?" I ask genuinely worried.

"Elizabeth, that is not why I called," Allegra sounds more and more annoyed. "I saw Frank in Aspen."

"Oh my God, what happened? Did you sleep with him?" Now I am totally distracted. I have this rule with phone calls, or more particularly returning them. Kitty called yesterday and left me a message. Because she does not call two to three times daily like Allegra, she gets put on a waiting list. When I actually sit down to return phone calls, she will be first, but in the interim, if Colby, Allegra, Mimi or Pippa call, they go directly to first place—make sense?

Turns out Allegra again escaped the clutches of Frank, and I have to dash to The Vassar Show House. Kitty and I are the welcoming hostesses for the day. We volunteered this year. Although I still have not figured out why we do The Vassar Show House, because we went to Lake Forest College. I do have an aunt and cousin who went to Vassar.

"Hi, Kitty," I say smiling as I walk in to the house. "Sorry I didn't call you back."

"Elizabeth, did you get my invitation for PAFA?" Kitty asks.

"No, why? What is it for?" I say knowing it is to be on the committee. Husband is simply going to kill me. All these invitations add up, but I hate to be left out.

"I want you to be on the young friends committee with me. It is the first year they are doing it. It's for the huge 200-year anniversary blow-out," Kitty seems excited.

"Of course, whatever you need. Who else is going to be there?" I ask to keep the conversation going. Kitty and I are not doing a good job greeting at this Show House. We are too busy gossiping and catching up. This is the Kitty I love and want to be friends with. I like our chats.

"The usual suspects. By the way, what are you wearing to Academy Ball?" Kitty asks.

"Oh, that is top priority for me. I have no idea," I say truthfully without bothering to ask Kitty. Even if she knew, she would not tell me because she would not want me to copy her.

"Where did you get your suit?" Kitty asks, this isn't a compliment trust me.

"Ann Taylor," I answer. So MC of me, I'm sure she thinks. It is a lovely beige cashmere shift dress with a matching coat the same length as the dress. I wear brown leather coach pumps. "Allegra has a similar outfit but I'm sure hers is from Europe," I add.

"How is Allegra?" Kitty wishes she was Allegra.

"Allegra had fun in Aspen, and she saw Frank there. It's such a small world!" It is. There are ten people in it and they all know each other somehow. I sware. It does not matter where you go, you can always meet someone who know someone you went to college or high school with. I love it!

"Is he rich?" Kitty asks.

"I get mixed signals, but you know, medium rich. I think he has a nice-sized house, nice car, a house at the shore and never worries about money, but if he spent it, there might be trouble," I say, assessing the details I have heard. "He has to work, let's put it that way." I end. We always categorize wealth. If you are rich, that just means you have nice things. You earn a seven figure salary. If you are medium rich, you are well off but you can't buy planes and vacations for the rest of your life. Having two to three homes would be normal. Medium Rich means a 10 million dollar trust fund. If you are wealthy, then you could never possibly go through the money you have. You make 250 million dollars a year. This type is quite eccentric, so we probably don't know too many of you. This is the most normal Kitty and I have been in a while and it is nice to catch up with her even though I know she is watching me. Plus, I wonder what committees she isn't asking me to join.

"Allegra is a strange duck," Kitty says carefully, knowing how close we are. "She is not very socially ambitious. Does she ever sit on any committees? I would like to keep her in mind." Kitty asks. *This is so funny!* I mean, in Kitty's world, she is generally confused by Allegra's apathy. Of course, I could use this as an excuse to take digs at her pathetic existence and shallow being, but I decide to take the high road.

"Well, you know she is single, and when you are single sometimes hanging out with a bunch of stay-at-home married mommies isn't that fun. Plus, she works, so it's hard to make the meetings." Self-deprecating humor works well in these types of situations. I learned that from media training when I was in PR.

"So other than Frank, does she have any prospects on the whole marriage thing?" Kitty is jealous of Allegra. I can tell.

"I think Allegra finds the whole dating thing amusing most of the time. I know she would ideally like to meet someone, but it would be pretty hard to fit into her world. I think that intimidates men. Allegra is by no means an SC," I say carefully, never wanting to trust Kitty. I can never tell her the true feelings of anguish Allegra feels.

"She is so amazing, and I know she will meet the right guy. When you are an AT, men can find it intimidating. It's hard to be alone." Kitty's eyes well up.

What the fuck is wrong with this girl? Crying on cue. "Kitty, what's wrong?" I ask.

"Nothing, I just hate for anyone to be alone, and just the thought of it... I mean, I love Allegra. I have such fond memories of her from college even though we aren't that close now. I just want her to be happy." Kitty dabs her eyes. *Right.* This is too dramatic. It's so typical and irritating. Kitty is jealous of Allegra because of her SS and couldn't give a shit if she is alone.

"Don't worry, Kitty, she is fine." I look for the bathroom. Turning to one of the employees I say, "Excuse me, which bathroom would you like us to use?" I ask, needing an escape. Kitty and I have such a strange friendship. I mean, when we are together we get along, but then she totally slights me other times. I can't understand it. I try to be nice to her and be fun to hang out with, but she just does not like or trust me. Why can't I get past it and accept that we are not going to be close friends? One minute I think, okay, we are on the right foot, and then other times, I hear she had a dinner party and did not ask me. *Why do I care? Note to self:* work on not caring what others think of me.

As I come out of the bathroom I notice Kitty is getting her picture taken and is just finishing giving her name, again. *God, don't they have it memorized by now?* That women from PAS is by her side again. *Shit!* She looks so familiar. Why can't I place her? Maybe Kitty got a Kenny. Lucky duck! I wish I had a personal assistant.

Then Kitty turns to face me. OMG Kitty has on the exact same citrine as mine. I have never noticed it before. *When did she get it?* Major distraction.

"Want to go have a cigarette" I say to Kitty as I walk toward her.

"Yes, definitely," Kitty smiles. *That ring. That ring.* When did she get that ring!

"I'll get them from my purse," I say seeing the tears are completely gone.

"Where should we go?" asks Kitty.

"There is a deck out back where no one will see us," I reply. Do I ask her about the ring? *No.* We're getting along now. I don't want to rock the boat.

"Like I care what anyone thinks," Kitty says, assuredly.

"Okay, then let's just go," I say, getting annoyed that this is becoming a production. For someone who does not care, hiding in the woods in the freezing cold seems ironic. Plus, she brought breath mints. *Typical!* Hiding deviant behavior just makes it seem more deviant. Own your smoking habit!

On the way home from The Vassar House, I listen to "Photograph" by Nickel Back. If my life had a soundtrack this would definitely be on it!

SC CARS:

Lexus SUVs

BMWs- all of them

Jaguar X class

Audi A4

Mercedes C class

Volvo S40

Land Rover (if you can't buy a Range Rover, don't drive one at all)

Lincoln Continental

Lincoln Navigator

Lincoln Aviator

Cadillac Escapade

Toyota Forerunner

Maserati

Mustang

Rolls Royce

Corvette

Lamborghini

Bentley Azure

Aston Martin

Porsche Boxster

Camaro

Volvo Station Wagons (If I never see another one of these as long as I live, it will be too soon)

Chapter XXVII

BEING LEFT OUT

"Elizabeth?" Colby can't totally hear me as the girls scream in the background.

"What's up, Colby?" I ask as I sit in my lace bra and underwear and stare at my closet.

"How are you?" Colby is polite but I know she has something to tell me.

"I'm good. I have nothing to wear, but I'm good," I answer. "How are you?" I ask back.

"Good," Colby says in her cute main line lockjaw. "Did you get your invitation for The Pennsylvania Ballet committee?"

WHAT? No! Must be cool. "No, when did you get it?" I ask.

"Yesterday."

"Maybe my mail is slow. Is Kitty the co-chair again?" I say, snidely.

"Of course. I did not get a committee list so I have no idea who is on it, but I assumed she would ask you," Colby says feeling badly if I am left out. She really wants me to be the co-chair of the Ballet. She's knows how honored I'd be. Even if I should focus on other aspirations and dreams.

"Quite frankly, Colby, I cannot handle another responsibility even though I love the ballet and have supported them for years. I even take the boys to The Nutcracker. I think Husband may leave me if I do one more event," I say, exasperated. "But the least she can do is ask since I am her ever-devoted slave on Academy Ball and some young friends start up for PAFA," I add.

"Don't worry. I promise not to have fun if you aren't on the committee," Colby says cutely.

"Thanks, honey. It just pisses me off because that is one charity I devote a lot of personal interest to. Besides dancing ballet for years, I still enjoy attending. I mean, honestly, when was the last time I heard the orchestra, except the times I am forced at opening night and the performance for Academy Ball? That girl just pisses me off," I am on a rampage. "I just spent a whole day with her last week for Vassar Show House, and she acts like I'm her best friend. I hate how deceitful she is! Now I'm mad!"

"Don't be," Colby says, being rational. "She's such a UB, and you know you two have never really been close. She's not a real friend to you."

"I know. It's just aggravating. It's like she uses me when she needs me and then the rest of the time I'm not good enough or I'm *persona non grata*," I say, feeling frustrated as usual with my on-again off-again relationship with this UB.

"Elizabeth, she is a weird girl. Don't give it another thought. You are a much better person than her," Colby says supportively.

"Thank you, you are such a good friend. Let's talk about something else entirely. I want to change the subject, but I do have one last comment. I know not everyone likes everyone *blah, blah, blah* but this is getting old!" I say, truly meaning it. I don't handle being left out well.

"Let's see, my husband is being evil again," Colby says moving on.

"Why, what happened?" I say concerned. Colby is great, a pain-in-the-ass type A, but great.

"Well, he told me if I wanted to go to the Art Museum event, maybe I should get a job to pay for the tickets and the babysitter." Colby stops, waiting for my reply. It is hard to sympathize. Husband would never say that to me.

"Did you remind him that the connections you make at these events are good for his practice?" I say trying not to be unsupportive or judgmental.

"No, that's a good one. I will remind him of that next time he puts me down," Colby says.

"How are the renovations?" I ask Colby. When Colby isn't running her daughter's school she decorates room by room. I think she will be done soon. Before the holidays is her goal.

"Great. I will show you when it's all done." *Yes she will.*

"I can't wait!" I say.

"Elizabeth, the girls are into the cookies again so I have to run," she says as we hang up.

What am I going to wear? I am so uninspired. I need a diversion, and then I will start over.

I go downstairs to blow out the candles. I always have cinnamon candles burning in the kitchen during winter. I love the house to smell like the holidays. I decide the green candles should be moved into the dining room where they match the décor better than the kitchen. Good! I love when I make a genius decorating decision on my own. I just saved money, because believe me, the decorator (Nicole) is the next person we will all have in common! Now I can go pick out an outfit. My new self-esteem will be helpful!

Why would Kitty leave me out of the one committee I really want to be on. I desperately need to work on this "not caring about other people" thing. My desire is to be self-actualized.

SPOTTING AN SC MAN:

Fake tan (cream or booth)

Monogrammed cuff links

Monogrammed shirts- (especially casual)

Custom suits

Wear their polo shirts with the collar up

Tie a sweater around their neck

Play golf & tennis (and not for the exercise)

Love Vineyard Vines

Wear Nantucket Red pants all summer

Wear wide whale corduroys with whales or any animals on them in the winter

Only wear blue blazers

Love Jazz music

Signet Rings or Family Crests

Drive like Mario

Have fake hair

Read Page Six

Ride Horses (only because it is prestigious)

Get manicures and pedicure- (secretly of course)

Work out all the time

Watch what they eat

Play in a band

Are excited to be on committees

Reads The National Review, Forbes, Fortune, Barons and WSJ (and uses its initials when discussing articles)

Does not know what sports radio is

Waxes

Knows what Daily Candy is

Look and save the pictures of themselves in the paper

Display pictures of themselves everywhere– (home, wallet and office)

Have lock jaw

Look at themselves in the mirror constantly

Check out the 18-year-old debs (short for debutante)

Wear Ralph Lauren aftershave

Use Clinique for Men face products–(only Penhaligon's or Trumpers)

Vilebrequin bathing suits

Ballroom Dancing Class

Watch: Patek Philippe, Tag, Breitling, or Rolex

Are named Jack

Chapter XXVIII

THE TEA CLUB

I have a theory that life never surpasses the 7th grade. When I was younger, I could not wait to grow up. Sadly, adulthood is similar to high school, or worse, middle school.

It is my month to host tea. I planned my outfit with Kenny the night before. I'm wearing a demure dress (Oscar) with an empire waist and a tiny bow giving the appearance of a belt. I accessorize with silk shoes with a bow to match, leopard of course, and lots of pearl jewelry.

I worked out with Nicki in the morning and my abs hurt. Good! Having children does a number on your stomach. Nicki is mean to me. She makes me work hard. My masseuse gets a hug when she leaves my house. Nicki once asked why I never hug her, and I replied, "Because I hate you by the time you leave." I don't really hate her as I watch my body get back into shape. I am grateful.

I am in a fabulous mood today and am really looking forward to my turn to host tea. It is my debut. I am also feeling very guilty at what an expensive wife I am. I remember Daddy saying to me, "Only a fool would support your clothing habit." Well, I've found just that fool. Husband is a love. Clothing aside, between $150 a week for my trainer, $350 a month for my masseuse and facial, $50 a week without tip for my mani and pedi and $250 a week for the chef service, Husband has his hands full. Husband is a good sport, and he kissed me good luck before he left this morning. Husband and I never discuss the UB, or anyone else for that matter. Husband just knows how to make me happy. Things. Husband gave me a sign that says, "Every Woman Needs Four Animals in Her Life: a Jaguar in the garage, a Leopard on her back, a Tiger in bed, and a Jackass to pay for it all." *Very Funny!* But I have it all. Sometimes I just don't realize it.

The doormen at The Rittenhouse greet me as I walk into the lobby. "Mrs. Quinn, you look lovely today," Martin comments.

"Thank you, Martin, so do you," I flirt back with a big smile on my face. Doormen are the best invention ever. I first fell in love with doormen when my college boyfriend used to have me to his parents' for dinner at their co-op in Chicago. Once doormen know you, you get VIP treatment. They open your car door, carry your bags and compliment you. They are an overall feel-good profession. There should be more doormen. I wish I could have one at home.

I arrive one hour prior to my tea to make sure everything is set up properly. Of course, it is not. "I asked Evantine to supply red roses. And was this carpet vacuumed?" I am trying to be as pleasant and polite as possible to the event coordinator, Anne.

"I will check on that right away," Anne says, quickly turning. It is winter and red looks really nice next to my complexion, especially because I wear so much ivory. Plus, the roses look great with the décor of the room.

I begin to put out the gift bags. The Rittenhouse is a lovely hotel for tea. They have a beautiful private room off the lobby with formal furniture and china. The layout of the tea is magical, and, of course, the wine is butlered. No one feels as if she must get up for a refill. Your glass is just full again, instantly. Soothing, classical music plays softly in the background. The staff wears black, and even the linens match the oriental carpets. I dine at The Rittenhouse frequently with Allegra. That is how the staff knows me so well. Plus, every bridal or baby shower I have ever hosted has been there. When I am in the city, I always park there and use their powder room. They have a full length door; very private. One could have sex and no one could see. Although I believe that The Rittenhouse is one of the premier hotels in Philadelphia, I still carry pens only from The Ritz Carlton. I have a whole stash.

Kitty, of course, is the first to arrive. "Elizabeth, hello," Kitty says, air kissing me. "Your dress. Is it Duro Olowu?" *Who?* Is she always going to do this to me? True to form the question is not a compliment.

"No, Oscar," I smile and signal for the waiter to get me a drink. Kitty is wearing leopard too. Figures, but hers is probably Valentino. *Why is she challenging me every chance she gets?*

"Who's coming?" Kitty asks.

"About 30," I answer looking for the waiter.

"Wow, that's a lot!" Kitty sounds surprised that so many people would attend a tea I am hosting. *I am not the enemy, or am I?*

"How are the girls?" I am trying to make conversation. I am sick of always being the one to fill down times with conversation.

"Perfect," Kitty smiles. Thankfully, wine arrives with Allegra. Kitty and Allegra say hello to each other. When it is your tea, you are allowed to invite people that are not formally in the tea club. Thank god Pippa could not come due to a work meeting, I did not need to set Kitty off. She is already out to get me with that dress question.

"Excuse me. I have to use the ladies room before everyone arrives," I say to Kitty, while glaring at Allegra that she had better join me. On our way to the bathroom I swear I see Mimi's fiancé going into the men's bathroom, but it isn't exactly the time to look and make sure. "Allegra, Kitty asked me if I am wearing Duro Olowu. Who is she?" I look desperate.

"She is a he, and he's the hottest new designer around. I am sure you have one of his brightly printed dresses and don't even realize it," Allegra says, smiling, trying to make me feel better. I breathe a sigh of relief; Kitty is always trying to belittle me, I swear. I have a bigger diamond ring, so therefore, I win! (Even if mine is slightly flawed, it is still larger).

Tea is magnificent. Everyone seems to be enjoying herself, and the conversation is flowing. I am on cloud nine. Except, Colby brought a friend from out of town that is wearing jeans—*um, hello?*

I see Mimi speaking to her fiancé and another gentleman by the front door. Good, I am not losing it. It was him. Mimi looks upset and stressed. I wonder what is going on? She walks right to me. "Can we go into Smith and Wollensky?" I think I see tears.

"Of course, sweetie, let me just tell Anne so she knows where to find me," I say quickly feeling a little panicked. I scan furiously for Anne. I worry *what is wrong with Mimi.*

Inside Smith, Mimi has ordered her signature martini. "Did you see Fiancé?"

"Yes. I saw him go into the bathroom," I say carefully, looking at her to try to gauge what is going on. I am trying to be comforting, but also since I am dying to hear what happened, I don't want to say anything to piss her off and shut her up. I love drama. My life is boring.

"Was he with anyone?" Mimi asks very seriously.

"I don't know. Let me think. Maybe there was someone in front of him or behind him but I was not paying that much attention because I was not one hundred percent sure it was Fiancé," I say carefully. I try to act innocent so as to collect the best data.

"Elizabeth, I think he's cheating on me." Mimi looks down.

"No, I never saw a woman," I swear with certainty.

"No," Mimi says softly, "I think he is gay."

Shit! This is huge. "Why do you think that?"

"He told me he was in New York for business today, and when I saw him here I nearly died." Mimi pauses. "He is always with that guy, George. They don't even work together, but I just figured they are friends for business." I say nothing, waiting for her to continue. "George seems gay to me, but I figured Fiancé had a good reason for spending so much time with him." Mimi sips her martini. I have the listening thing down due to Allegra and Colby. "Have you ever heard that the bathrooms here are a gay hangout?"

"Mimi, I don't know, but I doubt your fiancé is gay." We're in a hotel he could of gotten a room. And the bathrooms here are private.

"What time did you see him go in?" Mimi asks.

"Tea started around 4:00, so it was just around then."

"I just saw him leaving at 4:45. What were they doing in there? Elizabeth, our relationship is so peculiar. I know you hate to talk about sex, but he can only come if we do it doggy style." Mimi stops. I feel sick. This is weird. "And he watches a lot of porn and masturbates." Mimi stares at me with her big green eyes.

"Mimi, he isn't in New York. He's hanging out with a business associate. Why does that make him gay?" I am choosing my words so carefully. "They could have been having a drink to discuss work." Justify, rationalize and try to help, that's my policy.

"Elizabeth, I am about to get married, and I have a bad feeling about Fiancé," Mimi finishes her drink.

"Let's get back to tea and let this settle. We will go to Rouge afterwards and figure this out. For now we won't jump to any conclusions." Mimi and I walk back to tea, but all I want to do is pay the bill and get out of there. I am sad for Mimi. This is crazy. The problem with Mimi is her family is so well connected. She attracts all types of SC men. Why are so many gay men in politics, and why do they have to hide it?

As I am closing up my tab and waiting for Mimi to leave for Rouge, Kitty walks up. "Where are you off to?" Kitty looks lonely. I am caught off guard.

"Rouge, do you want to come?" Praying she says no.

"Yes, I would love to, but I have to use the bathroom first," Kitty adds.

"Go ahead, I'm not sure what we are doing. No rush," I say trying to buy time and get out of this. Mimi walks up in her gorgeous ivory cashmere coat with the chocolate sable collar. "Shit, Mimi, Kitty wants to come with us," I say trying to be forgiven.

"No fucking way! Let's just go." Mimi grabs me as we run out the door. We are running away from her. This is so middle school.

"Well, we can't go to Rouge now because she knows that's where we're going," I breathe as we run through Rittenhouse square. Mimi's plan is to figure out fiancé. Mine is to plan how to overcome Kitty.

"Brasserie is good. She won't go that far," Mimi huffs. Jogging in stilettos is hard work. I definitely need some Chardonnay psychology, which is what we call it.

Allegra informed me later Kitty was digging through the gift bags. Probably taking all the good samples from Kiehls. Allegra still thinks Kitty's ring is a fake!

Chapter XXIX

How Scs Shop

I cannot believe Christmas is almost here. Number one, Greye's school is making a big deal about Christmas being called Christmas. I am finding this very annoying. At Greye's school it is called "The Holidays." We will play by the rules. Christian children wish they could celebrate their other friends' holidays, like Chanukah. It's like the whole phenomenon of Christian children wanting Bar Mitzvahs! I just don't think the schools should ostracize people's beliefs and celebrations. You can't pretend Christmas does not exist.

Anyway, I am totally stressed because, of course, both Mommie and Daddy want to spend Christmas with Greye and Field. Husband is an orphan now, his parents both passed away. I am up to my eyeballs in shopping, and pretending to entertain--I'm not very domestic. I have 16 coming for Christmas dinner.

My wrists even hurt from carrying all the shopping bags with my bangles on.

I call Pippa for some much needed Saks and sizzle. Neither Colby nor Allegra are available. "Pippa, it's Elizabeth, where are you?" I plead.

"At home. Why, where are you?" Pippa sounds interested.

"I am at Saks, but I hear they serve Champagne at the restaurant. Can you come?" I am begging, while trying to sound cool at the same time.

"I'll be there in 15." Pippa hangs up. It's so easy to make plans with friends without children. I remind myself to make more of them. Pippa arrives as I order my second glass.

"What are you having?" I say, graciously thankful that she has arrived.

"My usual, vodka with a slash of club," Pippa smiles at the waitress who looks distressed. Pippa has that "It" quality. Pippa is wearing a lovely ivory cashmere sweater, very demure. It has a ruffled effect around the sleeves, neck and hem, but not Southern belle, old-lady like, very cute. She is wearing ivory silk cigarette pants and black velvet Kate Spade slippers with an ivory buckle. Becoming a Pew has done wonders for her wardrobe. "Only kidding," Pippa adds, "whatever she is having."

"I am in the worst mood. I hate the holidays," I frown.

"Don't you mean Christmas, little Miss PC," Pippa says laughing.

"What am I going to get Husband? He does not care about cashmere sweaters or silver cufflinks." I say. Husband is more of a sailing, hunting, fishing kind of man. We already have all the boat accessories we could possibly need. Matching Towels, shirts, hats, sweaters and those little cups you put your beer in. All monogrammed with the boat name: *The Mighty Quinn.* Husband also likes Bob Dylan and the Grateful Dead. *Don't ask.*

"Let's go to George's and get a real drink and figure it out." Pippa gets up, determined to get me out of my funk. Not for everything, but sometimes I need a NR to rescue me and put me back in my place again. I mean come on, I don't even cook! Let alone for 16 people, even if half of them are children. I follow Pippa, driving a black Mercedes E class, down Montgomery Avenue. Was this named for Mimi's family, I wonder?

When we arrive at George's, Pippa smiles as she orders us Chardonnay and lights my cigarette. Thank god we can still smoke in Pennsylvania. It is banned in New Jersey. That's another reason I don't hang out there. "So I don't think Mimi is liking her fiancé right now," Pippa says.

"Why," *Is there more?* I must confess, I love dirt!

"Well, apparently, he is way sucking up to her family but nothing else if you know what I mean." Pippa looks serious.

"That's terrible. I mean your sex life should at least be good while you are dating." I so want to change the subject now that it is about the sex thing and not a good fight. I think the whole Duncan debacle turned me into a prude. Plus, I don't want to share what I know. "Are you going away the week after Christmas?" I ask, dying to know where a Pew goes.

"Actually, we're going to Jackson Hole in Wyoming." Pippa is treating me like an idiot. I know what state Jackson Hole is in.

"Oh, I've never been, but hear it is amazing." I recover because, of course, this is a true statement. *Who does she think she is? It's me, after all.*

"We're also skiing in Stratton with Mommie, which is perfect, because she is the only babysitter I trust." This is falling on deaf ears, and Pippa looks bored because she does not have children yet. "So what are you wearing to The Academy?" I ask.

"I'm not sure yet," Pippa says. *Is she not sharing?* A good friend does not keep secrets. Very Pew of her, I think.

"Should we attempt JM with a buzz" I say, smiling, but also wishing I had called Mimi. Allegra and my theory is that Pippa has an inferiority complex with me. She wanted to be the first married, a total NR wish. It's easy for me to say that. I was the first married and the first to have children. Pippa also feels really left out when Colby and I talk about our children. Being a Pew is the only thing she can hold over my head. Sometimes it works.

"Let's do it," Pippa smiles as she pays the bill.

Do friendships really change this much when you aren't both in the same boat? I wonder as we pick out gorgeous scarves, gloves and silk pants at JM. Maybe I just hate the holidays. I used to love them when I was growing up, but now that I have two children it just isn't fun any more.

I wish life were like an L.L. Bean catalog, where everyone looks happy and warm, even in the snow. It would need a soundtrack with it. Music is the spice of life. I've always wanted to be in an Eminem video. They look so fun on MTV "Making a Music Video." And in that TV show Ally McBeal, her therapist told her to have a theme song. So she could go to a happy place when she was feeling scared. *God, Ally McBeal was neurotic.* "Where the streets have not name," by U2 plays on my radio. I listen to loud music on the way back to the shore, smoking the whole time. To make myself feel better I decide to take the boys to see The Nutcracker, even if I am not on the committee. I went every year when I was little. It is tradition. I love tradition!

Later at home, "Hello?" I say, answering the phone.

"Hi, it's Mimi."

"What's up?" I ask.

"Nothing, I am wondering when the next committee meeting is?" Mimi asks.

"I can't remember. Do you really want me to check?" I ask.

"No, don't bother. I'm just bored. What did you do today?" Mimi asks.

"Shopping and drinks with Pippa," I say.

"What? That bitch! I called her yesterday, and she has yet to return my call!" Mimi sounds jealous. *Here we go again.*

"How is Fiancé?" I ask, treading lightly.

"Okay. You know, majorly kissing my ass. Swearing up and down he loves me and only me." Mimi exhales loudly.

"Did you ask him if he is gay?" Getting right to the point. She needs to know.

"I did. He was shocked. Then we had sex that night so he could prove his point." Mimi pauses, and then adds, "I am not 100 percent convinced. But things are better." She sounds drained from the whole thing.

"Good then. You will keep me posted. Have you spoken to Kitty?" I ask, changing the subject.

"No, I'm trying to avoid speaking to the UB until after Academy Ball, so I don't have to hear about how busy she is."

"I know, it's nauseating. I should go, Field is getting cranky, and I need to give him a bath."

"Okay, call me when you hear about our next meeting." Mimi hangs up.

"It" girls love to shop. Colby and I are driving to New York City to hit Bergdorf's. I am determined to find a pretty cocktail dress that no one has seen in Philadelphia, in *Vogue,* or on Kitty. On the way up, Colby and I plot. "So how many events do we have?" Colby has brought a stack of invitations.

"Opening of the ballet, and PAFA," I read "but you can wear short dresses to both of those," I add.

"Okay, that's perfect. So then it's two parties and then Academy Ball." Colby counts in her head what she will need. Academy Ball is mandatory full-length gown.

I, on the other hand, being on the committee, have an extra cocktail party. I can't even worry about Academy Ball. The preview parties are around the corner! "I hear red is hot this year! I look lovely in red, so that is my goal," I say with determination. "Should we hit Canal Street for fake Chanel bags?" Colby asks.

"But, of course," I say enthusiastically. "It will be our secret."

Later at Bergdorf's, Jill, the sales woman, helps me as Janine carries piles of dresses following Colby. "This will look perfect on you," Jill says pulling the red strapless Carolina dress from the rack. I eye all of the racks and then settle into my dressing room. Nothing fits, I am in a horrible mood. I must call Nicki the minute I get back from New York, I need to up my workout sessions, as I can't be fat for Academy Ball. It is a major event. The Bellevue has five floors for the party. Each floor is decorated in a different theme and has a different band. The top floor is the premier floor. That is where Oscar will be. They are having major security. Only people that paid a certain price will get into the top floor. The Lester Lanin Band will be on Oscar's floor. I doubt I'll bother even trying to get in, even if I am on the committee. The Young Friends, us, are in the basement. Kind of like at home. Except my children will only play in the basement when their friends are over. Otherwise they must be by one of us at all times—talking non-stop. I know where they get that "talking thing."

Chapter XXX

PERSONAL TRAINERS

I sip water as I wait for Nicki to arrive. I drink Penta water all day long. It is a great detox, and it is good for your skin. I try to ingest only things that are good for my skin like vegetables, nuts and blueberries. Somehow wine and cigarettes still win out at night. "Hi," I say as Nicki enters.

"Hey," Nicki says. "What are we working on today?"

"My entire body! I am feeling so fat," I complain.

"All my clients are saying that to me today," Nicki says handing me 20-pound weights. "Alternating lunges first." As I lunge, Nicki asks, "Do you have an event?"

"I have a committee cocktail party for Academy Ball," I breathe.

"New Moon on Monday," by Duran Duran plays on my iPhone.

"Same with Britta, my other client," Nicki says. I know Britta Pew. She is Pippa's adorable sister-in-law, who I am confident hates Pippa from what Mimi told me about the gift situation. "She is pissed today,"

Nicki adds. I do not want to spoil the dirt so I just sort of crinkled my face to ask why. "People are unbelievable."

"Go on," I say.

"Her sister-in-law is really abrasive. Apparently, after their Mother passed away last year, she expected half the jewelry, bags, clothes and furniture. Britta was wearing a pair of earrings from the estate to see if she liked them, and this girl practically ripped them out of her ear." Nicki pauses. This is awesome, unbelievable and so usable I am practically forgetting how hard I am sweating. "Then she and Britta were at a shower for their cousin's wedding, and her sister-in-law's gift was from the estate, a silver tray! Britta was so upset that she left the shower pretending one of her children was sick. To add insult to injury, she was covered in the fur, clothes, bag and jewelry she took from Britta!"

"What an SC! This girl sounds awful," I say, trying to remain calm. Poor Pippa.

"That's not all. She apparently never buys Britta's children any gifts. Yet, for this cousin, who is now pregnant, she sent a congratulations gift as a total kiss-up," Nicki exclaims.

"Honestly," I say out of breath. "That girl sounds like a total SC. Britta is such an AT, she should ignore her," I say.

"Yeah, that's what I pretty much told her, but I was shocked when I heard that story," Nicki says, handing me 12-pound weights. "Try this weight for a shoulder press." Ugh, I really hate working out some days.

Chapter XXXI

COCKTAIL PARTIES

Wearing a black cocktail dress (*yuck*), I march down the street to enter Kitty's house for the Academy Ball committee cocktail party. I can't wait to find Mimi to share the story about Pippa. I love when I have dirt for Mimi because she always has better dirt than me. Husband can barely keep up with me. Mimi and I are the official staring committee for tonight's event so we can report back to Colby and Allegra. Nothing will top this dirt.

Kitty and Kit are nowhere in sight as I enter the house. They are probably having their picture taken by a society photographer. How can the papers be so interested in two people? The house, as usual, looks fabulous. I don't even care about Kitty tonight. Husband and I head straight for the bar. Of course, that is where I will find Mimi. There she is, looking adorably preppy and simple in a beautiful black pants suit. Very chic! She has her hair pulled back into a low ponytail with an oversized black silk scarf tied into a bow and big huge diamond studs. "Engagement gift?" I ask, giving her a kiss and a knowing look.

"Hi!" Mimi practically shouts, giving me the, "I'll-tell-you-later-put-a-lid-on-it" look.

"Shall we go outside and have a cigarette?" I ask as Mimi grabs her monogrammed silver cigarette case and matching Dunhill lighter. We dump Husband with Fiancé. Husband will be fine. He can talk about anything. Plus, Husband loves Kenny, so if Mimi's fiancé is gay, it will not bother Husband. That is what I love about Husband. He reads so much and is such a nerd, that he literally knows something about everything. I am so used to that. It was practically a pre-requisite as Daddy read the paper all the time and ignored me, but if I ever had a question he could answer it. It's such a great resource. You really never have to know anything. You can just ask Husband or Daddy.

Anyway, Mimi and I proceed out back to the sprawling flagstone terrace overlooking the countryside and light up. "So what's going on?" Mimi asks.

"You are never going to believe what Pippa did," I say, inhaling my Marlboro Light. I see Kitty out of the corner of my eye. She is standing too far to say hello. I can see her on her cell phone. *How odd.*

"What?" Mimi's interest is peaked.

"First you have to tell me how many carrots those diamonds are!" I demand. She can't get the gossip until I know how big those things are! Jewelry is such a distraction. I'm so superficial.

SOCIAL CLIMBER STYLE--FOR THE HOME:

Jonathan Adler

Assouline Books as decorations on the bookshelves

J Strongwater

Juliska

Waterford

Baccarat Crystal

Chippendale

Limoge

Herrend

Pierre Deux

Toile

Tufenkian rugs

Wedgwood

Niermann Wieks Lighting

Spode

Versace Dishes

Brunschwig and Fils

Donghia

Donghia Lighting

John Widdicomb

Stark Carpets

Baker Furniture

Duck Decoys

Oriental Rugs

Porthault Linens

French Decorative Arts

Claire Murray Rugs

Aubusson Rugs

Swaim

Saint Louis Crystal

Sevres China

Minton China

Lee Jofa

Hästens Bed

The Dux Bed

SC "It" Designers:

Alexa Hampton

Thomas O'Brien

Charlotte Moss

Bunny Williams

Diamond Barratta

Kelly Hoppen

Barbara Barry

Parish–Hadley

Brian McCarthy

Mario Buatta

Barry Dixon

Barrie Spang

Nate Birkus

Whitney Cutler

Chapter XXXII

How Socialites Ski

Stratton bustles at the holidays. There is an adorable village full of shops, restaurants and a spa at the base of the mountain. Mommie's town house is there too. My absolute favorite is The Wine Bar. The least expensive glass of wine is 18 dollars, most are in the 40 dollar range. People from New York City have insane amounts of money. They don't care. Husband won't mind if I only buy one. We arrive two days after Christmas. It gives me an extra day to try to organize all the new toys and put away the dishes. Husband drives as I don't drive trucks. They are too large. We need the truck for this trip. Husband has a Forrest Green Tahoe. It has a third row in case we bring another family. But mostly its useful as Greye and Field can watch the television in the back. Greye's obsessed with surfing movies this trip. In between Field and Greye is a large bag filled with game boys, toys, books and snacks. They look adorable staring at the screen with their headphones on.

We get to the mountain for first run. Greye is in ski school, most days Field's home with Mommie. She skis with us one morning, Mommie knows friends that will nanny. Judi is the nanny today. I only ski until lunch. The day Mommie skis with us she organizes a picnic in the lodge with all of the "trail blazers," a.k.a older gentlemen who get discounted rates on lift passes and free valet for their skis next to the gondola. They are so cute! Mommie's friends have all of that old fashion Austrian type ski equipment and outfits. The Stratton Mountain boys play the chicken dance in the background and yodel. I love Stratton!

"World Cup was the best run today," Mommie observes as she sets the table, with silver. Mommie is wearing a light blue ski suit that makes her blue eyes pop. Mommie loves pastel.

"I liked Spruce, it wasn't as steep," I add. Mommie and I love to dissect the skiing. I am wearing her mink sweater with black stretch pants. Very Audrey Hepburn.

"You are skiing well Elizabeth," Mommie compliments. Skiing was more important than school. Skiing well, in my mother's book, is next to godliness.

"Thank you," I say helping her put out the pâté and stuffed mushrooms.

"Do you like the K2's you demo'd?" Mommie is obsessed with skis. I demo'd Lotta Luv's. Mommie owns Sweet Luvs.

"I really do!" I mean it. I felt strong out there. My poles are pink and green. Mommies are white.

"What time will you be home?" Husband is fetching Greye to have lunch with us. Mommie will put the baby down for a nap after lunch. She takes one too.

"Four thirty. Then our dinner reservations are at six o'clock." Mommie won't go out for dinner. She can't smoke. And Mommie *has* to have a cigarette with her cocktail. I just stand outside by the fire pit. Husband joins me.

"Where are all your friends?" I wonder.

"Any minute. Is Colby coming for lunch?" Mommie loves Colby.

"No, I am meeting her at the spa." Cold mountain weather is extremely drying. One must get a facial after flying and skiing. Then we have cocktails.

"Sit and eat," Mommie hands me a linen napkin. She is very bossy about eating and she's still my mother after all, even if I'm one too. Greye and I both have low blood sugar. If we don't eat every three hours we are grumpy. I am a *Baby Wise* mother. My sons are on a strict schedules. Breakfast at 7:30, dressed by 8:00—it takes 20 minutes to feel full and I want them eating slowly. Snack as soon as Greye is off the bus and dinner by 6:00. Baths are at 7:00 and bedtime is 8:00. I go to bed at 9:00 and I need an hour to myself to set up for the next day. It didn't really work anyway. *Baby Wise* promises if you keep them on a schedule and get them sleeping they won't cry. That's a lie. My son's both cried till they could talk and needed to be held 24/7 until they could walk.

After our spa appointments we head to The Wine Bar. It is all glass so you can see the mountain in front of you. The fire smells delicious. We get a cheese and fruit tray with our wine. "How is your house?" I ask Colby. She had it redecorated complete right before the holidays. I haven't had time to go see it. I'm sure it looks lovely.

"I love it. I am really proud of the wallpaper in the foyer." Colby smiles pleased with herself. "It" girls have gorgeous homes.

"Nice coat," Colby says admiring Mommies mink.

"Likewise," I say with a twinkle in my eye.

"Tarzan Boy," by Baltimora plays on the stereo.

"When's the housewarming party?" I joke. *Let's get back to the house.*

"Seriously," Colby sips her wine. She won't have one trust me. Her husband is an ass and Colby wouldn't want her house to get trashed. "Oh my god I completely forgot to tell you!" Colby has dirt. *Yeah!*

I nod sipping my delicious Chardonnay wanting to hear the story.

"I had a ballet committee meeting at my house for Kitty, something going on at her house I can't remember," Colby pauses. "I didn't want anyone upstairs, I had everything set up in the living room." *Who goes upstairs at a committee meeting?* "Kitty marched right in and gave herself a tour of my entire house." Colby is annoyed.

"She's been decorating her house forever. I'm sure she wanted to check out what you did to make sure it's not better than hers." What an SC.

"I had even put potted plants in front of the stair cases and in front of doors to rooms." *That's a little much, these people aren't criminals.* They're on the ballet committee for god's sake.

"Did she knock them over?" *Can you imagine?* I can be funny occasionally. I am not a joke teller. Well I do tell one about a fan in heaven and masturbating. But usually Mimi tells me I'm funny when I am being dead serious.

"Literally I felt violated. I could hear her commenting to Bryn about my rugs and drapes. Like I need her approval." Colby wants her approval, trust me.

"Total novice move. SCs don't get it," I say. *I want to see it now!*

Chapter XXXIII

THE SPA

"It" girls go away to the spa to detox, not rehab. During the first week of the New Year, I check into The Greenhouse for fat flush. I have so much stress that I am starting to feel dizzy and lightheaded. Of course, Husband told me I need a multi-vitamin and some sleep. I decide to do that, but at a spa. My stepmother couldn't go with me. She's co-chairing some children's cancer gala. *Great! Now I'll have to go to that too.* The Greenhouse is in Dallas, Texas. The limo driver recognized me immediately at the airport. He didn't have a picture of me or even a description, but as he said, and I quote, "You look like you are here for The Greenhouse." How could he have picked me out of hundreds of people?

They lock the doors behind you when you check in. It is a lovely establishment with a formal living room, library and dining room where they play the piano every night at dinner. Ladies wear cocktail attire, but no cocktails are served. At least not the kind I am used to,

Chardonnay. They have cranberry cocktail (unsweetened and diluted with water). It helps flush out the system.

Morning begins with breakfast in bed at 6:00 A.M. The guest rooms are lovely suites overlooking the pools. There is one outside and one inside. The sheets are Frette or Pratesi, and the amenities are very plush. After breakfast you go for a brisk walk. It is good for the lymphatic system. Everything at The Greenhouse, especially during fat flush week, is good for the lymphatic system. I spent seven grand to care for my lymphatic system. Next you stretch and another workout class follows. One day it could be a workout with weights, another it could be traditional aerobics or a dance class. At 9:45 you get a potassium broth break. They also serve carrots and celery with your broth, but you are only allowed one of each. Beauty treatments follow: facials, scrubs, detox wraps, massage. Lunch is served by the pool. The other guests and I are all still in our robes and slippers. Lunch is fish over salad with fruit for dessert. We go back to beauty treatments in the afternoon: manicures, paraffin, pedicures, saunas, steams, hair and make- up. A leisurely yoga class is offered in the late afternoon with a frappe (a.k.a. a very small fruit/protein smoothie). Late afternoon is free time in your suite, while you are starving, reading a magazine and preparing for dinner. Dinner begins with appetizers in the library—a cucumber slice. Everyone is dressed!

During evening appetizers, I am getting the skinny from the group gossip, Wynn Whittington, who has already been here for a week. "There's a child star from "Growing Pains" here. She is trying to launch her career again, so her agent has had her here for over a month to lose weight. I think she used to be a drug addict," Wynn adds, "You never see her. She stays in her room and barely works out. Every now and then you'll see her come get her broth. It's the only thing they won't bring to your room here," Wynn adds with a twinkle in her eye. Wynn, a true Southern belle from Texas, has the perfect Southern accent. I cannot figure out why she is here. She has platinum-blond hair, blue eyes and looks to be a size four or six. Maybe she is having a nervous breakdown like me.

"So are you here to relax?" I ask.

"Yes," Wynn says strangely. "Then there is the St. Louis snobby socialite, Susan." Wynn changes the subject. "She is very tall and thin and no one can figure out why she is staying here. Maybe she is detoxing from more than stress. Michelle, the masseuse, told me she keeps wine in her suite."

"There's a girl after my own heart," I say with a smile, although I don't mean it. I drank too much wine, if there is such a thing, during the holidays. I am exhausted, and all I want is my dinner. I cannot figure out why I have to sit in this stuffy living room making conversation while sipping ice water with lemons. "Are they always this late?" I ask.

"Yes," replies Wynn, "always." I am intimidated by Southern women. They are so poised. And they always know the right thing to say. I could have never made it at SMU.

Thank God I am only staying until Wednesday. I have to get back to do last- minute follow-up for the ball, but three days will be perfect for me to loose a few pounds for my dress and de-stress. Dress, oh my

231

god! I don't have a dress! How had I not thought of this? FUCK! Okay, first thing tomorrow, I'll get a car to take me shopping. "Wynn, where does one shop in Dallas?" I ask.

"Oh, darling, you must go to Stanley Korshak," Wynn says assuredly.

Later in bed, I toss and turn. Even though you get a detox sleepy bath and then a tuck in massage on your back and feet. I'm as restless as can be. All I want is a good night's sleep, but all I can think about is the dress. I am obsessed.

The next morning I phone the concierge. "After morning workouts, I will need a car."

"Yes, Ma'am. What time, Mrs. Quinn?" the concierge asks. *They are so Southern,* I think.

"1:00 P.M., directly after lunch. Thank you." I have to be deliberate, and I also have to ask for a rush on alterations and fast shipping. This will be close. I can pull it off.

I am lucky enough to find a dress in a size 8. They hem it in one day and FedEx it to Margate. Perfect! It is not that fabulous, but it looks great on me. It has a long straight skirt and the cinch around the waist that is flattering, so I am happy. It is black, so not a real stand-out dress, but I don't need to try to compete. Just getting by is my policy at this event. Super wow will be my goal for next year.

The next day at lunch, Wynn saunters into the dining room. "Hello," she says enthusiastically to the group. Everyone smiles and says hello back. She is "Miss Personality," and everyone loves her. She sits right next to me. "So, what did you do this morning?" Wynn asks me.

"Oh, the usual, I stuffed myself with vegetables and flax seeds, worked out, slept in the sauna and had another facial," I say with humor. "My husband is going to die when he sees the bill," I add humbly.

"What does your Husband do?" Wynn asks.

"He is an eye surgeon," I say. "What about yours?" I ask, figuring she has left the door wide open. I would not usually ask, but since she started it… On the Main Line it is looked down upon to be nosy about how one earns a living. We usually just tell each other either before or after the introduction is made. For example "The Quinns, whom you just met, he is an eye surgeon."

"He's in oil," Wynn adds coyly. *Oil? That's convenient.*

"Thank you for the shopping referral. I loved SK, and they were so accommodating," I say graciously.

"They are the best," Wynn says with a smile. "Are you on a committee?" Wynn asks knowingly.

"Yes," I say weakly. *I will probably not be for much longer.* Kitty was a real UB at our last meeting about the raffles. Halloween has not helped matters.

"Okay, ladies," our evening speaker begins. "I am here to discuss the latest and greatest in sneakers this evening." She has a bunch of truly ugly sneakers displayed with a huge poster of an African person standing with a stick. "Masai Barefoot Technology is the answer to your thighs needs," she says with a smile. "These sneakers will transform your legs, butt and stomach." She continues, "The unique imbalance of the platform forces your muscles to work harder to maintain your balance, therefore transforming your workouts and making them four times harder."

Hmmm, a sneaker that looks like an orthopedic shoe that will make me thinner. I LOVE THE GREENHOUSE! I will be the first with the MBT shoe, albeit ugly. I will wear truly ugly shoes to have thinner thighs.

The next day I sit in my room, starving. As I apply a clear coat to my manicure and pedicure (it makes it last longer), I debate what to wear for dinner.

That evening, Susan, the St. Louis socialite appears. After many evenings icing her face (some kind of procedure), she deigns to join us in the dining room. Maybe she is out of wine. I am getting a Kitty vibe. Putting my lack of judgment aside, I sit next to her. "Where are you from, Susan?" I ask politely, intentionally digging.

"St. Louis," Susan coos back in her drawl. One-word answers! Charming! I wonder what her husband does.

"I love your necklace," I say, glancing around. I begin noticing everyone is wearing dazzling jewelry. I suddenly feel inferior. "I left my nice jewelry at home," I add humbly.

"So did I," Susan says smugly.

That's it. I am not talking to another UB as long as I live! I go to bed that night even more determined to put my past behind me and move on from this world full of mean people. I just don't want to care anymore. *Note to self:* go to Amazon for books on self-actualization. I will become genius in the art of being nice and attracting niceness!

I leave the next morning two lbs lighter and six inches smaller. Goodbye starvation! Chardonnay, here I come! I feel refreshed, relaxed and ready to handle the ball. Plus, I cannot wait to see the babies. Greye's porcelain skin and Field's soft pillow cheeks make me homesick for my family. Field still has dimples on the back of his hands, elbows and knees. I will be sure to kiss each and every one. I order a glass of wine on the plane.

SC Diets:

Atkins

Rancho La Puerta

Fat Flush

Skinny Bitch

Golden Door Spa

South Beach

Clinique La Prairie

The Sonoma Diet

Anything by: Oz Garcia, David Kirsch, or Gunner Peterson

Mayflower Spa

The Zone

Canyon Ranch

French Women Don't Get Fat

Miraval

Martha's Vineyard Diet Detox

How The Rich Get Thin

We Care

The Skinny

The Wall Street Diet

Not:

Jenny Craig, Nutra systems, LA Weight Loss, Bob Green (Oprah's guy), You on a diet, Medi Fast, Slim fast, The cereal diet, Suzanne Somers or Weight Watchers

Chapter XXXIV

HAIR, JEWELRY, THE FIGHT, THE CONFRONTATION

"It" girls have the best hair. The Academy Ball is only weeks away so I go to Pierre and Carlo to get my hair done. I am sitting down in Peter's chair, and he says, "I saw your friend, Kitty, last week."

I respond, "When?"

He says, "Oh, she was in getting her hair blown out." I think, *probably getting more extensions added to her hair.* Nobody's hair is that thick!

I say, "Oh, that's great! I love Kitty." Meanwhile, I'm thinking, *Kitty is on my last nerve.* I would never say that to Peter. Of course, I must act as if she is the greatest gift.

Peter says, "Yeah, she said that she's been really, really busy with the committee for the Academy Ball, and she's been having a lot of problems."

"Really, what kind of problems?" I say.

"Well, apparently the person in charge of her raffle committee sucks and has been doing a really bad job. Kitty is so mad at her that she is going to see that she is black balled from all other committees ever." Gay hairdressers love to be dramatic, and are always in the know.

My heart sinks, my face is burning, and I am starting to sweat. She was talking about ME! I look at Peter and say, "but *I'm* in charge of the raffle committee. She must have meant me."

Peter looks really embarrassed and says, "Oh, Honey, No, No, No, *No*, it isn't you. She was talking about another girl. Kitty loves you. She was saying how great you are. I know it definitely isn't *you*." But, I know it is me and he knows it, too.

I am so embarrassed, but I try really hard not to look any which way, to keep a stoic expression on my face. Thank God that Botox has left me expressionless. I say, "Yes, I know you are right. Kitty told me that I'm doing a great job. I'm sure it isn't me. Don't even worry about it, Peter." So, quickly I try to think of a way to change the subject. I ask, "What are you doing this weekend?"

As I leave Pierre and Carlo I am in such a bad mood I can't even hold the door for anyone. I just pretend I do not see the person behind me. Ugh, I am such a bad person. I hate The Bellevue! I hate all of the snobs. No wonder this place had to be shut down due to a disease! In the 1980s, the hotel was closed because of Legionaire's disease. It was a sign the whole place should have been burned to the ground! I race home after my appointment, walk in the door, don't even say hello to my children, throw down my purse, pick up my phone and call Colby immediately. Dialing her number I am raving mad. She finally answers.

"Colby, it's Elizabeth." I am practically barking each word.

"Hi! How are you?" Colby clearly had a good day.

"You are never going to believe this!" I huff.

"What?" Colby says innocently, but nervous.

"I was getting my hair done, and Peter told me that Kitty had just been there and said that I was the worst raffle committee co-chair. She's going to make sure I am black balled from being on all other committees in the future," I stop.

Colby is silent....

I say, "Can she do that?"

Colby says, "No, never. That will never happen, don't even worry about it." I can hear the relief in her voice. She is glad it's not her. Even if she does feel badly for me.

"I'm fuming, Colby. Who does she think she is? I have worked my ass off on that raffle," I exclaim.

"Of course, you have. You've done a beautiful job. It's going to be an amazing raffle. You got the Four Seasons, the Ritz Carlton, and The Rittenhouse Hotel. Don't worry!" Colby is trying to be supportive.

"Colby, I hate Kitty Kimmel. I swear to God, I don't know who she thinks she is. Just because her in laws' own Barneys, does not give her the right to be so imperious! She hasn't done anything but boss people around." I am so over this UB.

Colby reassures me: "I know, I know. Don't worry about her. You are so much better than her. You are so much nicer. People are just nice to her because she's rich and has SS. You are prettier, and you have a better life. So, don't worry about it." I don't have SS. My family doesn't own squat.

"How can I not worry about it? She's out to destroy me. She hates me for some reason. Why does she hate me so much?"

Colby says, "She doesn't hate you! Just try to put it out of your mind. Focus on your beautiful children, your beautiful life, your beautiful home and your wonderful husband, and try not to focus on Kitty." Colby adds, "You know what they say: Living well is the best revenge."

I say, "You're right, you're right. I'm going to get a glass of water and sit down and not think about it. After all, what can I do? I can't make people like me. If they don't like me, they don't like me. Not everybody likes everyone, right?" I feel desperate. Who is she saying this too? If she is saying it to Peter then she is telling EVERYBODY!

Colby says, "Absolutely. Don't worry about it. This is not the end of your social life."

"Okay, I've got to go, I think I hear Field crying." I hang up. The baby isn't crying. I am still so angry! Why doesn't she like me? What had I done? I had worked tirelessly, and she is just cunning. She gets everybody to do all the work and didn't need to do a thing. Plus, she is taking all of the credit. I worked my ass off. I cold-called strangers and asked them to donate things. I put blood, sweat and tears into this raffle and into being on this committee. After all, it is the ultimate to be on the committee. Instead of water, I poured myself a glass of J Lohr Chardonnay. Chardonnay psychology, down the hatch!

I can hear Husband pulling into the driveway. I am so angry with myself. Why do I care what she thinks about me? Why do I care so much? Yet, I am so hurt. I do seek her approval, and I do want her to like me. I want her to put me on all of her committees. For some reason, nothing else seems more important at the moment. I can't wrap my mind around it. I have everything I ever wanted: my health, my family, my beautiful home, and none of it matters. I feel so shallow and pathetic and I hate myself for feeling this way. It's an icky, icky, yucky feeling! I feel guilt and remorseful, as if somehow I have done this to myself, Karma, The Duncan thing? But what have I really done? I need to stop thinking about it and instead need to make a massage appointment.

Husband walks in the door. I feel ashamed and embarrassed. I do not want to tell him, but being really upset is written all over my face.

Husband says, "Hi! Honey, how was your day?"

I say, "Good."

He says, "What did you do?"

I reply, "I got my hair highlighted and blown out."

He says, "That's nice," while reading the paper on the counter.

I say, "Kitty Kimmel said that I am doing a bad job as co-chair of the raffle committee, and that she is not going to put me on any committees ever again."

Husband replies, "Kitty Kimmel is a crazy bitch. Why do you care what she thinks or says? Anyway, you are on too many committees as it is. It would be good to take a break and maybe save some money." Then he smiles.

"I know, I know. You're right. I'm going upstairs for a little." I turn and walk away.

So, I go upstairs and smoke a cigarette. I realize that the best thing to do would be to watch "It's a Wonderful Life," because at the end of the day, everything I ever wanted has always been right here. Just like in the movie "The Wizard of Oz," there is no place like home. I have two beautiful children. I love listening to my boys talk to each other in their cute little voices, I could cry. I love the way they say they love me. I love being home on a Sunday morning, reading the "Style" section of "*The New York Times*" and the "Image" section from the "*Philadelphia Inquire,*" and drinking coffee with my husband while the boys play with their make-believe boats and trains. I love drinking Chardonnay at outdoor cafes like Devon in Rittenhouse Square with my friends Colby and Allegra, talking to my father and torturing him by making him watch horrible MTV Reality shows, talking about skiing with my mother, and discussing fashion with my stepmother. All of these memories help me to realize that it doesn't matter what committee you are on, or how many parties you go to, or what your SS is. At the end of the day, I have everything. Now I need to focus on that!

Allegra's grandmother always says that it only takes one generation to create a fortune, but it takes three to create a gentleman (or a lady in this case). At this rate, even Kitty's daughters will be wretched. *Poor Things. Kit will save them.*

The next day I wake up refreshed and prepared to confront Kitty Kimmel. I have to get it off my chest. I can't have her running all over Philadelphia saying I am a lazy committee person. First, I do twenty minutes of weight exercises and then go for a jog. It is very important to do weight training, cardio and also, stretch. I usually do yoga because

I like it so much better than Pilates. Pilates is too much the craze. I do it, but I secretly hate it and say nothing. After I get back from my jog, I put away the dishes and the tea towels, throw out the beer bottles from the night before, put away all of Greye's Legos, organize the shoes underneath the bench, fold the laundry and put in a white load, fold all of Field's blankets and organize all his stuffed animals facing forward in a cute pile, raise everyone's shades perfectly in the middle of the window, because I want them just right. Nana has Field at the library for story time. Then, I make myself breakfast. I make cooked oatmeal, not instant. That is what Jennifer Anniston, I read, eats everyday, and she looks great. I then check my emails and get back to everyone promptly. I then do fifty Kiegel exercises because my doctor said it is good to do them all day long. Then I warm up the shower, put my gym attire in the hamper, lay out my lace underwear and bra, pick up a pair of stacked heels from Gucci and a cute sleeveless sweater dress in winter white. It has a matching cashmere long sleeve sweater coat to go over it. The dress is Bloomingdale's brand, not designer, but I am a pro at copying all the latest fashions from my hours of studying fashion magazines. Yes, I will admit it; I don't just read fashion magazines for the articles. If I am going to see Kitty, I am going to look beautiful. In the shower, I wash with L'Occitane cooling cucumber soap and matching body wash. I only exfoliate once a week on Sundays, because it's with a very scratchy brillo pad-like loofah that almost hurts. So, I can only stand it once a week. However, I do scrub my feet with a pumice stone every day. I wash my face with a glycolic wash, because you must exfoliate your face so that your skin looks younger. I don't want to look old now that I am in my thirties. Since I just had my hair blown out, I don't need to wash it so it is tucked up in a headband. When I get out of the shower, I pad dry with a rough towel, to further exfoliate for younger-looking skin. Then, after toning with Kiehl's herbal cucumber, I use Vitamin C serum, an emollient, a matching skin and eye cream to detox and reduce circles around the eye, and finish with some Murad energizing pomegranate lip therapy on my lips to keep them supple. Then I apply a final layer of spf to protect my skin. I do not put on lipstick till the last possible moment in the car because lipstick can be very drying, especially with a lip liner. I apply a thin layer of Burt's bees lip balm in raspberry for anti oxidant protection. You do not want to put too much gloss on your lipstick because that will make it soft and it will just get all over everything and run into the cracks of your lips. Then I brush my eyebrows so that they are all neat and standing up, and, I use a Crabtree and Evelyn's Gardenia lotion because it complements nicely with my Carolina Herrera perfume. I use Dove cooling cucumber deodorant to enhance the soap I use. I finish by putting a little powder on my underarms in case I get extra worked up, angry, or hot and start to sweat. I don't want to smell. For this I use Crabtree and Evelyn's baby powder. Then, I put on my outfit and brush my hair fifty times with my Mason Pearson brush because Mason Pearson is the best for hair and makes it extra shiny and full. I put on my pearl earrings with matching triple-strand pearl necklace and bracelet that Husband got for me in China. I put on my Coach tank watch, my engagement ring and my wedding band (of course, I have a four carat emerald cut and the band is from Tiffany's, engraved from my Husband with his initials and mine). I also decorate my right hand with a pearl cocktail ring.

I come downstairs and get my Jacques Ferber sheared mink. We know Kitty buys sheared rabbit and lies about it. Ooh! I am so mad at her! It has my hot pink initials on the inside for flavor. Tone on tone looks best, but when you open up a beautiful coat like this and see bright pink initials, I think it is funny. Hot pink and green is my absolute favorite color combination in the whole world. But neither color compliments my skin so, I can't wear it. If I could paint the world pink and green, I would. In fact, I only plant salmon-colored flowers in my garden in the summer because it offsets the green trees surrounding my house.

I get into my car. If you can't have the nicest Jaguar, they now make the affordable lines like an Audi, or a Mercedes that produce any of the cars that you really want for about $35,000. They are only a bit smaller and a little stubbier than the luxurious kind. I drive to Philadelphia to meet Kitty at Craig Drake where we are picking out our jewelry for the Academy Ball. Since Kitty is the co-chair, and I obtained a raffle item from Craig, our exclusive jeweler at the event, we are allowed to borrow jewelry for the ball. Nice perk!

On my way, I call Allegra for moral support. I say, "Allegra, this UB is being really mean to me."

Allegra says, "Oh, fuck her!" I can hear the noise her Hummer makes. As European and classy as she is, she still drives one of those big, Hummer cars. She has Kelly Clarkson's Miss Independent playing in the background. I can hear her take a drag from her cigarette.

I say, "Allegra, pay attention. This is my life I have to live here. You are not from here, so you don't care."

Allegra says, "That girl is an SC. She is way too skinny, she is miserable, and she is probably still mad at you because you slept with Duncan."

"I know," I say. I keep forgetting about that. "Do you really think she still holds that against me? They dated when she was in high school. She should be over it by now. We're in our thirties! She's married and has children!"

Allegra says, with her Greek accent, "I know, but it doesn't matter. He was the love of her life, and you slept with him. Therefore, that makes you *persona non grata*, and she will hate you for life. It's called Karma."

"This is so unfair. I didn't even like Duncan. I was drunk."

Allegra says, "you were definitely drunk, and you shouldn't have done it.

But you did, and she is going to hate you forever, so just get over it. Move on."

I hang up the phone with Allegra. I do not like her right now. And her advice sucks. She is acting so virtuous. Think of all the men she has slept with! Allegra is always so matter of fact, even if she is right. Colby says advice can be given but it doesn't have to be taken.

I thought about it. I can move away. I could. *Maybe that's a bit dramatic.* My Husband can be a doctor anywhere. I have money from my grandmother. I can use that. I can rent a house for the summer. I'll just disappear for a couple of months with the boys. No one will even know I am gone. I'll just get through Academy Ball, and afterward I'll contact a real estate agent. I will look for houses in Blue Hill, Maine. It's lovely. I lived near there one summer. Oh, it is amazing how beautiful it is up there. I'll have the best time. The houses have tennis courts, pools, and pool houses and boats off the dock--and a guesthouse. At the main houses, cocktails were served in formal attire every night at five o'clock with dinner at seven o'clock. One would sit down to three courses and maids would bus the table. The maids wore traditional outfits with little white collars just like you see in the movies. Plus, you don't have to drag your trash to the end of the driveway. The trash men come into your garage and fetch it for you, so you don't have to touch the smelly trashcan. That is what I'll do. I'll live in Blue Hill! I love it up there. No one will know who I am. No one will know what I've done. I won't have slept with anyone's first love or love of his or her life. I won't have been a bad committee co-chair. I can just be fresh. Greye and Field can play on the beach and dig for clams, shells and sea glass. I'll get a light tan on my legs because I always like my legs to be tan. I would not dream of tanning my face. I use spf 50 on my face even when it's raining. I'll buy some clothes from LL Bean. *Well, maybe not,* but I can be really preppy. Husband and Greye can go fishing too. This is so perfect. I am so excited that I want to contact a real estate agent now. I hope it is not too soon. I must get a referral.

Armed with my new confidence about the prospects of my summer in Blue Hill, Maine, I march up to the showrooms of Craig Drake Jewelers. Once I have been gone for a while someone else will do something that everyone will be talking about. Everyone will forget about me. When I come back I will be fresh and since I will have been gone for the summer I will be missed and popular again.

"It" girls always get to borrow jewelry. Kitty, of course, is already in there and I can hear her talking.

"Oh, I love that, it's beautiful. You have the best taste, Craig. I just love you. You have the classiest collection." The trill of her voice is making me ill as I smile at the receptionist on my way in.

I say, "Hi, Pretty."

Kitty turns and says, "Elizabeth, I think this will go perfectly with my Roberto Cavalli dress. What do you think?"

Kitty has new boobs! I say, "Yes." I can't think. It is so beautiful. But I am completely distracted by the boobs. I have to focus. Craig Drake is an interesting jeweler. They do not have a storefront. Private clients only. Their store is in an office building off Rittenhouse Square, and they cater to businessmen and their wives. I say, "Hi, Craig."

He replies, "Hi, Honey, how are you?"

I say, "I'm good, I'm good. Just getting ready for Academy Ball." *Kitty has new boobs.*

He says, "Well, look around and pick out what you like."

Kitty keeps holding up things and asking, what do you think of this? What do you think of that? I'm wearing this color, blah, blah, blah. All the time, she is putting too much emphasis on herself. Kitty is wearing leather pants with a gold Hermès buckle. Tucked into her pants is a beautiful printed Nanette Lepore blouse. *Her boobs are HUGE!* And she is really skinny. Whatever weight she gained in the fall is gone. She looks stunning, but I am not going to be intimidated, at least not today.

Everything is beautiful and looks great, and Craig is being a perfect gentleman, doting on her. I walk around the showroom and don't even care what I am picking out. I usually live for jewelry. I can't hear her anymore and am thinking about what I will say. I have been practicing. So, Kitty picks out her jewelry and I, mine. We walk to the elevator and I say, "Kitty I need to talk to you about something."

"What, Honey?" Kitty looks un-phased.

"I heard that you said that I have been a terrible co-chair for the raffle committee, and that you are going to make sure that I never get on any other committees in Philadelphia." (I am very proud of myself. Sometimes I can be so articulate and say exactly what is on my mind with the exact level of coolness and confidence in my voice.) Then I just stop talking, forcing her to answer me. I learned that in PR too.

Kitty goes white, which is pretty hard because she is about as white as a piece of paper. Her skin is so thin you can practically see the veins. I am wondering what Duncan ever saw in her because she really isn't that pretty.

She says, "Elizabeth, Honey, No, I love you." Kitty hesitates. "You have done such an amazing job with the raffle committee. I was a little disappointed with the restaurants. You didn't get LeCirque, You didn't get Twenty-One, and you didn't get Le Bec Fin. I said that to you, and you accepted that."

I say, "Kitty, I got twenty other restaurants including Danielle and Nobu. Not everybody wants to be at Le Bec Fin. I think LaCroix is pretty nice."

She says, "I know, I know, I know. Oh my gosh, I know. You did an amazing job. I don't even want you to worry about it. I love you, and I am always going to put you on all of my committees. You did a great job, and we're going to have so much fun at Academy Ball. I want you to promise me that you won't think about this. Who said this to you?"

I didn't want to answer her. I didn't want to get Peter in trouble. "People are just saying it about me. And I was worried it came from you."

"No, it wasn't me. I know you did a beautiful job. You are a brilliant co-chair for the raffle and I will recommend you to everybody." Kitty is trying to be sincere but it's also condescending.

I say, "Thank you, Kitty." I do not mean it. I do not believe her, but I am glad I let her know *I knew*.

We give each other an air kiss, but I know deep down that she doesn't mean it. She thinks that I did a bad job, and I know that she is talking about me. I'll let it go because I got it off my chest. I said how I am feeling and I let her know.

At the end of the day, the most important thing in the world is not Kitty Kimmel, the Kimmel Center, the Philadelphia Orchestra, the Academy of Music, the ballet or the opera. Committees don't mean crap! What are important are me, my health, my parents, my grandparents, my husband, and my two beautiful boys who love me. I have a beautiful home, wonderful friends and what more can I ever possibly ask for in life? Now I am ready to move on.

On the car ride home "Turn this mother out," blares by MC Hammer. It's illegal to talk on your cell phone, while driving, in New Jersey. And I will never learn how to use a blue tooth. I will call Mimi immediately the minute I get home. We should keep a score sheet to see who has the best dirt. Kitty got breast implants. *Interesting!*

That night when Husband gets home, I tell him about my brilliant plan. I say, "Honey, I have a great idea for the summer. Why don't we rent a house in Blue Hill?"

Husband looks at me. "Okay, for what?"

"For the summer, for the whole summer, I'll take the boys up and I'll enroll them in camp. We'll rent a house, and we'll go fishing."

He chuckles, "You're going fishing?"

I reply, "You can fish and I'll cook."

He laughs again, "You'll cook?"

I reply, "I can boil a lobster and chill it on salad the next day. Plus, there are places up there that steam and crack the whole lobster for you." I stop and think. "We can bring Nana with us to watch Field and cook for us." Brilliant!

Husband smiles.

I say, "Seriously, Honey, I really want to do this. You know how much I loved summers in Maine when I was growing up. I want the boys to experience what I grew up loving. I'll try to find a house that comes with a Boston Whaler. It will be perfect!"

Husband just looks at me. He is always supportive and always agrees to do things even when it is not necessarily what he wants to do. He usually just gives in and lets me do what I want, which is so sweet of Husband. I would be lost without him.

"Ugh, can you open this baby food for Field. I just ruined my manicure," I wine. Even though I am being level-headed I still have a temper and take out my anger on my loved ones. I am trying to move on with this Kitty thing but need to yell at someone since I couldn't yell at her. Husband feeds Field. As I walk away I step on a cheerio. "UGH! Joan when will you be here next?" I say to no one in particular. It's not as if our cleaning lady can hear me.

So the next day, I phone the realtor in Blue Hill and she says, "Honey, I have so many houses for you. I will email everything over to you right away."

SC Scents:

Joy

Worth

Shalimar

Chanel No.5

Jo Malone

Giorgio

Gloria Vanderbilt

Carolina Herrera

Kate Spade

Anaïs Anaïs

White Shoulder

Vera Wang

Michael Kors

Calyx

Burberry

Lovely

Pure Tiffany

Obsession

Oscar

Creed

Anything by the following: Britney Spears, Paris Hilton or Jennifer Lopez (Glow? Need I say more?)

Chapter XXXV

THE PHOTOGRAPH

"Hello?" I answer, dreading the call. This is the first call from Kitty since the confrontation. *What can she possibly want?*

"Hi, Elizabeth," Kitty trills into the phone.

"Hi, how are you?" I say, trying to be nice, hiding my nervousness. *Where is this going?*

"I need a huge favor. The Academy cannot find anyone on the program book committee to attend a photo shoot today at Wills Eye Hospital. Is there any chance you can attend at 1:00? Someone from The Academy has to be in attendance," Kitty pleads.

This is an interesting proposition. Being on the program committee is very prestigious, and although I am not, it might be fun. "Sure, Kitty, I'm free. I would be happy to help," I say, meaning it.

"Great, thank you. The photographer's name is Glen. His cell phone is 215.681.0278. They will be in the lobby. You should have no trouble finding him. Thank you for doing this so last-minute. Oh, and by the way, they need you to be in the photo," Kitty says sincerely.

What? She must have called everyone and their mother before asking me. "Umm. Well, are you going?" I ask.

"I can't. I have something with the girls," Kitty replies. This is such an easy out for her. Children are the consummate excuse. I can't believe she would miss an opportunity to be in a picture. She must have something really important to do. Program book pages are expensive and hard to get into.

"Okay, no problem," I say, hanging up. What shall I wear? This is humiliating. I have my chocolate brown dress from last year, a Morgane Le Fay. It is really pretty. Perfect! Too bad Husband isn't working at Wills today, or we could have had lunch. I wonder if I am going to know the docs in the pic. I never even asked.

When I was a debutante the money we raised was donated to Will Eye Hospital. Will through a luncheon for us and we were given a tour of the hospital. It was to supposedly see what our money went towards. I guess that was kind of the first committee I was ever on. How funny. I never thought of that till now. I regret the day I started being on all these committees. Anyway now Husband says they still do that and all the docs sit their gawking and the pretty young ladies.

As I arrive, I spot Glen right away. I feel so stupid wearing a floor-length ball gown in the hospital, in the middle of the day. "Hi, Glen, I'm Elizabeth Quinn from The Academy Ball Committee," I say as I reach out my hand.

"Hello," Glen says in a friendly tone. He is busy setting up his camera with his assistant and checking for light. He hands me a piece of paper. "We received this agenda for the family photograph," Glen says, clueing me in that they are anal.

"Thanks," I say, reading the agenda. The photo is being taken in the Pew wing. Oh, God, is Pippa in this picture? I never even really noticed Wills had a Pew wing. No, it is not Pippa. It is her aunt-in-law, father-in-law and Britta's children. This is funny. Oh, and of course, the Mayor. Why did they need me, I wonder? Glen must be reading my mind.

"The daughter won't pose in the picture. That is why they asked for someone from the committee. You look lovely. Last time the committee member showed up in her tennis whites. That is very inappropriate. You will be standing here," Glen directs.

Just then the family enters. "Hello, Glen," Mrs. Pew trills. She is a typical WASP in a conservative Chanel cocktail dress with matching shoes and lots of pearls and gold jewelry. Trailing behind her is cute Britta and her children. They look so adorable. Mr. Pew is in a tux. The Mayor appears out of nowhere, and Glen begins arranging everyone. I guess the Mayor knows better than to be late for the Pew family. I can just see the title now: The Pews in Pew Hall.

I try quietly to do my job, "Hi, I'm Elizabeth from The Academy Ball. Thank you for sponsoring a page in this year's program book," I say, smiling.

Mrs. Pew looks at me and then keeps talking to Glen. "Glen, are you available the first week of July? We are having a family reunion in Maine, and I would like for you to take the portrait."

Glen looks up, thinking about his schedule. I know they go to Camden, so I won't see them. Thank god. "Sure, I believe I am available," Glen looks pleased. *There's never a dull moment.*

"How many years have we been doing this now?" Mrs. Pew says in her lockjaw. *Oh, please.* Should I even bother to remind her we met at Pippa's wedding? *No.*

"Let's see. When your neice was your grandchildren's age, I think," Glen says.

"Yes, it's been forever," Mrs. Pew drones on. *So what?*

As we stand and pose, I overhear Britta on her cell phone. "I hate her," she is trying to whisper. But I have very good ears and there's an echo. "She is apparently friends with a bunch of girls that are in a tea club, and they did not even ask her to be in it. What does that say for what they really think of her?" Britta pauses to hear the reply from the caller on the other end. "Oh, no, she told me she thinks they are pathetic, and that they are all a bunch of soccer moms getting drunk in the middle of the day," Britta adds. She is talking about Pippa, and what Pippa says about The Tea Group. I could ruin her with Kitty. If Kitty heard she said that, she'd see that Pippa is never on any of her committees ever, not that she is now. You know what. Who cares? I am not getting involved any more. Poor Pippa just felt left out. And let's face it, Pippa and her husband did not meet in an ideal situation.

"Thank you," Glen calls out. "I think I have it. That's a wrap."

I thank everyone again and practically run to my car. I do not want to be seen in my dress. Plus, even if I am not going to tell Kitty, I have to call and tell Mimi. I'm winning the dirt contest.

Chapter XXXVI

INVITATION STUFFINGS, GIFT BAGS, & THE RAFFLE

This is the busiest committee time ever. You literally meet everyday to get ready for this ball. I am exhausted. I have done nothing but pick up raffle items for the last week. First you go to the Academy and stuff all the invitations. It takes hours. Then you go back the next day and put everything into the gift bags. Nimis may have donated the bags and the items to go into them but the committee has to put them together. The Academy is gracious and always has cold water for us. I think I lost five pounds this week. Then once all the raffle items are collected the committee goes over to the Bellevue and sets them up on the tables. You need pens, and paper so people can write down their bid and all items have to be displayed just so. I hate being on committees! I don't care if it is prestigious. Plus, I feel like everyone is staring at me. Kitty must be bashing me to literally a bum on the street. I am paranoid.

During raffle set up I say to Kitty, "I am going over to 20 Manning to pick up the gift certificate, a menu to display, matches and whatever else I can get my hands on for her auction item."

"Thanks Honey," Kitty says on Percocet. Her girls are running around the ballroom. *Where are all her nanny's?*

Instead I say, "Do you need anything while I'm gone?" To that I do not get a response from the UB.

I greet Audrey Claire at the entrance to the restaurant. They are only open at night. Audrey is totally channeling Michelle Pfeiffer from the movie Tequila Sunrise but my favorite was Grease two. Cool Rider is like the best song in the whole world!

20 Manning is a big local hang out. Very chic. Audrey is sophisticated and beautiful—inside and out. She always has the best pony tails. I give her a weak hug. "Thank you so much for your generous donation." She gave me ten gift certificated for 100 dollars each.

"You're welcome. You look tired Elizabeth," I am. I did Audrey's PR when I was a publicist. We love each other.

"Well I'll see you at Academy Ball," Audrey hands me 20 Manning printed napkins along with the rest of the loot. Each display is truly an ordeal. You can't just pop a gift certificate on a table for Academy Ball. Each one has a lavish display. I'm surprised Chef isn't required to come and stand behind the table and make food.

My phone starts ringing. *It's fucking Kitty! What does she want me to do now?* She is being too pushing. I am going to crash. She probably wants me to run errands for her!

I answer, "Hello?" All I can hear is muffled noises. *Then*, it gets clearer. But Kitty's not talking to me; she's talking *about* me.

"She's a loser. She lives at the shore. She doesn't even use a decorator for her home. They're poor. She invited me to a Phillies game to sit in her Daddy's Diamond Box. Whatever. I sit in the owner's box when I'm at games." Her voice trails off. *WHO is she talking to!* I hear breathing. Then baby babble. Her daughters are playing with the phone. They dialed my number on accident.

I am shaking. My body feels hot. *What the FUCK!* She is still talking about me even though I confronted her! Do I have to talk to her about this again? I have to call Colby. I need Chardonnay Psychology. When will it ever end?

Colby answers on the third ring, "Hi, Honey. How are you?" Colby says in lockjaw.

"Bad! Kitty's girls called me on accident and I overheard Kitty saying I'm poor, I don't have a decorator, and she sits in the owners box at Phillies games. I'm a loser because I sit in the diamond box." I lay it on the table.

"OH MY GOD," Colby pauses. "Kitty is a UB. Elizabeth, honestly, this is the most toxic relationship. Stop being on her committees now. Steer clear of her company. Hang out with all your new friends at the shore." This is very direct for Colby. I feel like I'm talking to Allegra.

"You're right. I'm going to Maine in June. I'm done." I say feeling fatigue wash over my entire body. "I'm dropping this last auction item with the concierge and going home. I need a glass of wine and sleep." I say determined to never be in this situation again. I can't let people treat me like this. It's draining. I want to be home with my little boys.

"Perfect. You'll have fun at the ball. Go to Mimi's shower and then take one long, well deserved vacation." Colby makes me feel better.

"Making Love Out of Nothing At All," by Air Supply, blares on my radio as I smoke a cigarette on the drive home to the shore. Where I belong.

Chapter XXXVII

THE ACADEMY BALL

"Hello?" I answer the phone. "It" girls go to balls.

"Hi, poodle, it's Ken. How's the dressing coming?" Kenny asks supportively. He can't believe how mean Kitty is. Kenny is cheering for me.

"Good, I guess. I'm feeling pretty relaxed," I say, feeling tired. The whole ordeal is getting to me. I'm just glad this event is finally here and going to be over with soon so I don't have to think about it any more. "The UB called everyone yesterday to thank us for all our support," I add.

"You will be fabulous. Kitty is such an SC. Don't worry about her and have a great time. Call me tomorrow with all of the dirt," Kenny says and then adds "*Vogue* already called me to make sure they get your picture." Kenny jokes.

"I will. Thank you for calling. What are you doing tonight?" I ask.

"You know, the usual, something with Billy. Kisses," Kenny says as he hangs up.

When Husband and I arrive at The Academy of Music, we are late. I am nervous. It is looked down upon to be late to the concert. The biggest taboo is skipping it altogether. I didn't want to get any dirty looks. We are seated just as the speaker, Ocsar, is wrapping up. There's no real harm, although I would have loved to have heard what he said. I can see Kitty in the premier seat overlooking the stage. I, of course, am seated behind a pole. *Figures.* Kitty probably did the seating chart. I've decided to talk to her about "she's a loser, she's poor" incident tomorrow. I have to stick up for myself. But after that, no more Kitty committees. Since Kitty is not looking my way, I begin paging through my program book, despite "listen to the orchestra" looks from Husband. I just roll my eyes. I don't even like orchestra music. I know it's the oldest music hall in the country, but that does not mean I have to like the music they play to support it. I appreciate the importance of the arts and what they add to our community. What does Husband think I have been doing all year? Daddy just says I don't have an ear for music; that I inherited from him. I admire my picture at Wills. It is toward the back of the book. Not bad, I think. Pippa must be green with envy!

Everyone strolls down Broad Street from the Academy House after the concert to The Bellevue for the Ball. It is quite a scene with all the men in their white tie, tails, gloves and top hats. Some even carry walking sticks and wear capes. A band plays music. They close down the block. Bubbles are in the air like snow. It is truly magical. As we walk down Broad Street, the band is hopping. I can see up ahead the photographers snapping and Kitty and her boobs trying to get in every picture. I just hang back. No point in ruining my night. I duck into The Palm for a pre-ball cigarette. To my amazement half the committee is in there, toasted. They had not even gone to the concert.

The best part, so far, about Academy Ball is that Kitty Kimmel and Pippa Pew are wearing the exact-same dress from Roberto Cavalli. Kitty pretends that she doesn't care, but I know that it is killing her, because they are being photographed together all night. I know that is making her crazy. If Kitty is going to be in *Town & Country* it isn't going to be with Pippa!

The Academy Ball is beautiful. We are having a wonderful time. Kitty pretended that she likes me even though I know that she doesn't. She gave me a huge hug and a glowing smile when I bumped into her at the bar. Of course now, she is only talking to the men.

Just then, Mimi saunters over. "Did you hear?" she smiles devilishly.

"Uh, no, what?" I am dying. Good dirt will really help me right now.

"Kit Kimmel found out Kitty has been having an affair!" Mimi is still smiling. As she whispers, she tries not to let her mouth move or look too obvious.

"WHAT!?!" *I am so excited!* "How do you know this?" I exclaim and half yell, as quietly as possible.

"Kit was at The Philadelphia Club for their annual poker party, and Dr. Housel went up to him and offered his condolences on Kitty's abortion." The Philadelphia club is a men's only club. Like Pine Valley but without the golf. Women go to The Acorn Club.

"WHAT?" I am loving this too much. "Who told you this?" I plead in shock. Looking around trying to spot Kit or Kitty anywhere without being *too* obvious.

Mimi ignores me and continues, "Kit was so pissed off because clearly he did not know about this. He apparently went home and threw her out of the house."

I feel badly for her, but only for a minute. Only a minute! "So, how did he know she was having an affair?" I ask.

Mimi continues "Apparently they have not had sex in over a year. Kit suspected she was sleeping with her trainer because he called all the time. Eric, her trainer, was the boyfriend she was living with when she met Kit. When he confronted her, she admitted to everything. This is their last night in public." Mimi gives me a look with huge "can you believe it" eyes. "Kit is suing for custody of the girls."

"Oh my God! This is crazy, Mimi. Where is she going to go?"

"Apparently she moved back in with her mother, in Conshohocken." Mimi says *Conshohocken* very slowly. Mimi smiles the "could you die" smile.

"Her mother lives in Conshohocken?" I say astonished. Conshohocken is not on the Main Line. It's, how do I put this, WT.

Mimi nods. The Montgomery's practically underwrite the entire ball so she was invited to an exclusive pre-concert cocktail party in the ballroom of The Academy of Music. She must have heard all of this there. I'll have to remember to ask her if she met Oscar. *But who cares about that now!*

"But I thought she was little miss richy pants from Gwynedd." She lied about where she was from, how typical!

"That is all a lie, and Kit has been covering for her for years. Plus, her ring is fake. She would not wear the family heirloom Kit gave her. She thought it was too small. So she wore a fake diamond. She is a total SC that became NR, and is now single. Apparently Kit hired a publicist for Kitty to help her with all her society obligations," Mimi says with a wink.

Allegra has been *right* all along! I am beyond thrilled and everything is making so much more sense. That is why she is so nasty. This is why her birthday parties were never at her home, when we were little. Come to think of it, I have never been to her home when we were in school together. This is why the society photographers were all over her. It all made so much sense! OMG that is who that girl is I always see at events. I must of known her when I was a publicist. I am such an IDIOT! "Who paid for her to go to Agnes Irwin?" I ask, continuing with my conjecture.

"Who knows? Probably a grandmother." This, by the way, is not uncommon. Which is why we can so easily speculate. Lots of parents were not able to afford private school, but an AT grandmother was going to make sure her precious offspring went to the right establishments. It remained discreetly within the family. So that is why she needs sales people from Jacques Ferber to help her look rich…. "I heard," Mimi adds, "She's been letting the nanny and cleaning people go and using the money for hotel rooms."

My heart sinks. I feel guilty. I feel so sorry for her. She deserves for Kit to leave her, but I hadn't known she was lying about living in Conshohocken. Had I, I would have been more sympathetic. It is hard to be poor and go to school with wealthy people. I know what it is like to live on the Main Line with all those Lexus' and lockjaws. If she had not made me feel so sub-par, maybe I would have not been so bitter and happy at her misery. Now it really made sense that she has a vanity plate; only a girl from Conshohocken would do that!

"When was the poker party?" I ask. *How long have they been living separate lives?*

"Around the holidays. I guess. I'm not 100 percent sure." Mimi glances around. We've been whispering for a while and don't want to get caught.

Then Husband interrupts and asks me to dance. It is so nice not to have to worry anymore! We waltz to the orchestra cheek to cheek. Husband isn't the best dancer in the world but he knows how to fox trot. We learned during our ballroom dancing class for our wedding. Our song is "Love and Marriage" by Frank Sinatra. Husband wanted us to dance to Scarlet Begonias by the Grateful Dead. Thankfully it is undanceable. Looks like I won't have to call Kitty tomorrow or ever again for that matter. I cannot wait to get home and take my shoes off and really relax, for the first time in ages. Mimi takes the trophy of best dirt. She's the clear winner. I have to stop watching E! News, I am a nicer person. A wave of happiness rushes through my body as Husband holds me tight. Now, I *finally* get "It!"

Chapter XXXVIII

How To Throw A Shower

Spring is coming. I can't wait to get to Maine. The Main Line has been chaos since Kitty's fall from grace. My phone is literally ringing off the hook. I have to learn how to turn off my ringer. I am not talented when it comes to electronics. Mimi's bridal shower is today. We've been planning for over a month. It should be fun.

"Hello," I say taking Colby's call. What am I wearing, will be her first question.

"Elizabeth! You are not going to believe what my husband said to me last night." Colby sounds pissed.

"What?" *Oh god, I hope this doesn't take too long.* I am still not dressed.

"After drinking beer by himself in the living room for an hour he told me that I am ugly." Colby stops.

"You are so not ugly," I am almost laughing. She is adorable!

"I know, I don't even care if I am. But what an asshole!" Poor Colby her husband is getting worse and worse.

"Would you ever leave him?" I say gently.

"Yes, but then I would have to sell my house. I love my house. It's too much work to get divorced. Maybe when the girls are a little older." Sounds like a plan.

"I hear you. Colby I really have to get dressed. I don't want to be late." I say feeling badly I don't have enough time to flush this out with her.

"I know. I just don't want to talk about it at the shower. Can we have drinks at Parc after?" Good idea.

"Yes, you know Mimi will want to keep going." Thinking of poor Mimi. She is still not sold on Fiancé. And the wedding is in four months.

"Perfect, I'll see you there." Colby hangs up.

Driving to Philadelphia, Cinderella sings "Don't know what you've got till its gone," on the radio. I picked a cute outfit for today. A brown tweed mini skirt from Ralph Lauren and an ivory silk blouse from Jones New York. Interesting label considering Jones New York is actually located in Philadelphia. I have Wolford fishnets on and beige pumps from Nine West. As I thank the valet and pick up my car ticket Martin already has the door open.

"Mrs. Quinn, you look stunning." Martin smiles. I am wearing lots of ivory pearls. I a new mink wrap over my shoulders. A little present to myself now that this Kitty thing has been settled for me by God's intervention. Even if I am a "loser," live at the shore, and go to the "Diamond Box," I still have friends.

"Thank you Martin, likewise." I flash him a big appreciative smile. Doormen rock!

We planned Mimi's shower at The Rittenhouse Hotel. It's a no brainer and after everything I went through with Kitty I was not in the mood to be super creative. Mimi does not care. Mimi's policy is as long as she has a martini she is happy virtually everywhere. And I see she already has one. "Happy Shower," I say giving her a little hug.

"Thank you!" Mimi smiles. She is so easy. Nothing fazes her. Even a 50-person shower for a wedding I think might get called off. *Do you really have to return the gifts?*

"I'm going to say hello to Anne and then be right back to be with you. After you greet we will have cocktail hour. During tea you can open the presents." I am controlling aren't I.

"Great. I'll be here." Mimi stands with her mother so people can see them as they arrive.

I spot Pippa in an outrageously gorgeous blond mink! "Nice coat Pippa!" I yell.

"Thanks," Pippa smiles.

What the fuck is that for? I ponder. Furs are distracting. *Where was I going?* God Mommie hates it when I curse. She thinks it is so un-lady like. Mommie swares she can still count on one hand how many times she has said the word "Shit." I wonder if that includes when she was younger. But there is no point in arguing with Mommie.

As Mimi opens gifts I take a break from putting wrapping paper in a trash bag and head to the patio for a cigarette. Pippa takes my job. As I walk out I snag Bryn and Merrit whispering on the patio. "I bet I know what you two are talking about," I smile.

"How's our favorite Jersey girl?" *Don't remind me.* Merrit says not asking.

"Need a light," offers Bryn.

"I'm relieved frankly, She's a total SC." Merrit offers.

"I bet you are," I'm not saying her name first. Now Merrit can get into The Merion Cricket Club and The Union League.

"Kitty was torturing me to get her girls into Tarlton. I did everything I could but at the end of the day I don't make admission decisions." Merrit knows why they wouldn't let them in and I am not asking why. I don't care.

"Did you see her breast implants?" I ask.

"OMG," Bryn's eyes get big. "I did not notice. I was so floored she was sleeping with her trainer."

"I had a friend who got implants right before she left her husband. It was to attract a new man." Merrit explains. *Interesting theory.*

I am over this. I need to go make all the bows into a flower bouquet for the rehearsal dinner. *If there is one.* Instead, "I better get back ladies," I say as I turn and head for the door. Kitty's departure is relief to Pippa too. Now she can be in the tea group.

Mimi is hardly paying any attention to what she is opening. She could care less. Mimi keeps talking to Allegra about some basketball game they went to. I am going to be easy going like that. Pippa was a nightmare when she was engaged. She literally counted the dollar amount of every single gift she received. I thought Mimi was going to strangle her in her sleep. Pippa's stopped that now.

SC Vacation Spots:

Martha's Vineyard

Fire Island

Cape Cod

Croatia

The Hamptons

Mustique

Aspen

Block Island

Deer Valley

Dubai

Whistler

Jekyll Island

Anywhere in Maine

Palm Beach, Florida

Palm Springs, California

Bermuda

Nantucket

Newport, Rhode Island

St Tropez

Naples, Florida

Lake Como

Little Palm Island

St. Peter

Lake George (saying "going to the Lake" is irritating--specify which one)

Stratton, Vermont

Sun Valley, Idaho

Stone Harbor

St. John

Pebble Beach, California

Cabo San Lucas, Mexico

Four Seasons, Nevis

Lake Tahoe, California

Sea Island, Georgia

St. Barts

Pocono Lake Preserve

Virgin Gorda

Twin Farms

Taos

Turtle Bay, Fiji

Paris

Chapter XXXIX

THE AFTERMATH

I am learning about a whole new breed of SCs. Apparently, there are older women preying on widowers. The men are fairly well off and very lonely. They don't want a 30-year-old. They just want some companionship. The problem is, the men are so old that no one would want to hang out with them. They need nurses. Well, this breed of SC does just that, while complaining behind their backs what a handful they are. Just when their health goes to pot, they swoop in and marry the men on their deathbeds. BEWARE! I saw it happen first-hand when my Husband's family started fighting over money. Meanwhile, the only thing they care about is themselves. They pretend as if their first and foremost interest is their uncle and this money-grubbing woman stealing it from him. What they care about most is their own inheritance. Really! But I am so in tune with these things. Now I totally get "It!"

Months later the invitation comes for the Opera Gala, and my name is not on the committee list. Of course, the UB is the co-chair. Surely she had been asked before the whole scandal. That is okay. I have sworn off committees. If ever asked again, I will say "no," acting as if I am just too exclusive to be on committees. I will play hard-to-get, and then everyone will be asking me. I will still say "no," unless, of course, I get involved with a children's charity. That might actually make sense since I have children. Anyway, I am thinking about going back to work when Field goes to Pre-School. "It" girls have careers.

I am feeling very content, refreshed and renewed with my new sense of self. I know what my priorities are and what is important. Everyone has his own problems. Everything happens for a reason. No one was thinking about me. Kitty was always only thinking about herself and her messed-up life. The reason Kitty never let me get close to her was because of her psychosis. Life is a journey, and there is such a thing as karma. Plus, it totally helped that I read this great article about forgiveness. The writer said to do it for you. Anger and pent-up frustrations are bad for your complexion, weight and health. Anger ages you. Well, I certainly do not want to stay angry at Kitty and hurt my good looks. That would be counter-productive. The writer went on to say, "forgive out of selfishness." *Well, even I can do that.* All you have to do is try to put yourself in the other person's shoes (a.k.a. empathy. I *am* learning), and then when evil thoughts creep into your mind, take a deep breath, close your eyes, and say "I forgive." I will do anything, including forgiving Kitty, if it means fewer wrinkles.

I am feeling so self-actualized and confident. I suddenly do not care about who's who, and what their parents own—blah, blah, blah. I *honestly* couldn't care less what others think of me. It is very enlightening. I recalled the article that said that something one does not like about oneself is usually what they do not like in others. So, while I was busy being jealous and disliking Kitty, it was *me* no liking the *SC* in me. I am so smart now. I knew Maine would do wonders for me, and that I would be happy here. I also realize that what may seem bad to me or insulting is from my own perspective. Everyone has his or her own opinion. For example, I think calling someone an SC is a huge insult. Someone else may take it as a compliment. So there is no point in getting offended. I just keep saying to myself, give me the strength to change what I don't like and accept the things I cannot change. Another realization (part of growing up): usually when people are being nasty it is because they have something terrible going on in their own lives that is eating away at them. It is not personal. The meanness comes from a place of being terrified on the inside. They are just scared. I actually meet people like that now, and rather than feel intimidated, I feel empathy. I know what it's like to feel afraid, or not sure. I like not caring what people think. It is their thoughts, not yours anyway. This feels very freeing!

The house in Maine is adorable, white and Cape-style. All the houses in my community are close to each other, and we walk to the club house right on the water to use canoes and rent a Boston Whaler for the day or the weekend. We can have cookouts at the clubhouse. There are tons of other children. I've met so many other women my age who also summer here with their children. Nothing could be better than spending a relaxing summer with my boys! Everyone has cocktails in the evening. The weather is cool enough to wear sweaters and shorts with our Jack Rodgers. We can look cute and not be hot. It is beautiful. I love Maine, and I am happy here. It feels like home. We all cheered in the car when we crossed the state border. I saw the sign for Maine while listening to "One Good Women" by Peter Cetera. We were so excited!

People have to rent here for 10 years before they are allowed to buy. Then the starting price is three million. The people who live here are either on the red or the white team. When a baby is born or someone marries they are assigned to the team. It is taken very seriously. They have games on all the big weekends. One year a guy broke his leg playing War. Since we are renters, we get to be on the team for the summer, but then we are removed. I am white and Husband is red. I look good in both colors. The clubhouse has square dancing every Sunday night and blue blazers are required at Friday--and Saturday-night cocktails. It is a very fun place to live; just like camp for adults. I play tennis during the day with an instructor. I would never dream of playing with a person. They don't hit the ball directly to you. It's way more productive to play with an instructor.

Our second weekend here we decide to take the boys to the beach for cocktails. *OMG* there is Kit Kimmel! I recognize those broad shoulders and blond hair anywhere. Plus, I see the girls. "Kit!" I yell out as he turns.

"Hey! What are you doing here?" Kit smiles a huge smile.

"We are renting here this year. You?" This is major.

"My Aunt and Uncle have a place. I brought the girls here for the week. They are done school." Kit's still is smiling as he and Husband shake hands.

"You should come for dinner with the girls. They can play with Greye and Field and we can catch up." I offer.

"We would love to, just name the day." Kit says.

"How about tonight?" Let's get this happening as soon as possible!

"Sure, what time?" Kit asks.

"6:00?" I throw out there.

"Okay then. You guys don't mess around. We'll go home and get cleaned up." Kit says and begins to gather their bags and shuttles the girls' home for showers.

Kit arrives with a bottle of wine. *Poor guy.* This must be hard being the Father and wife. Husband probably does not even know we bring hostess gifts. "Thank you, my favorite Chardonnay," I greet everyone at the front door.

After situating the children with snacks, games, the movie "Nemo," and arts and crafts I join Kit and Husband on the screened in porch for cocktails. They are discussing sports. I place shrimp cocktail on the table. The seafood is the *best* in Maine.

Dare I ask? Of course I do. Trying to be sensitive with a look of concern on my face I ask, "How's Kitty? Is it okay to talk about?"

Kit looks down "Yes, absolutely. Honestly I think she has a border line personality disorder." Kit's not finished talking but he sips his beer.

"She's living with her mother now. I don't think that is going to help the situation." Kit has a serious look of concern on his face.

"Why, what is going on?" Kit knows none of us knew about the Mother in Conshohocken.

"Her mother is a great lady. Kitty's dad left, when she was little, with his secretary and left her mother with nothing. Kitty's grandmother helped pay for school but that was all she could afford. Kitty's mother got a nursing degree and went back to work. It was rough."

"But why did she hide it. She should be proud of her mother for keeping it together." She sounds like a strong woman.

"Kitty's mother made her work and give some of the money for the bills. She really resents her mother. Kitty's mother had to work a lot. She wasn't around much." Kit pauses to take another sip of beer. "Maybe she was a little neglected. I agree she should respect her but that's what I mean about her mental state. Kitty would blame her mother for her father leaving. She despised her mother. I guess she was ashamed," Kit opens another beer.

"She is very self absorbed." I know.

Kit just looks at me and then finally says, "Yeah she was rough on you." A smile almost breaks through.

I *knew* she was talking about me but to Kit! Husbands don't care about girl drama. "I don't mind. Sounds like theirs a lot to the story I didn't know. Maybe she was trying to have a better life than the one she grew up with." I do feel bad for the girl.

"It's more than that. She would lie all the time. And about stupid stuff. Like, she would say she had lunch at Barclay Prime and then my buddy would say he saw her at Christopher's in Wayne." Kit pauses "She screamed at the girls a lot too. Lost her temper very easily. She never would spend any time alone with them. It became so obvious she was having an affair. But at the point I didn't care. She would work out at night and then say the traffic was too awful and would use one of the rooms at the Racquet Club and spend the night." Most private clubs have a few rooms you can use.

"Yes, I went to a few of the happy hours there, but I never saw Kitty," I add.

"Their is so much more. I really tried to help her. At night, she would go into the girls' room when they were asleep and kick the bed until they woke up. Then she would say, "You girls don't love your mother" in a drunken stooper. Like, a psycho mommy dearest. She agreed to go to therapy but would lie to her therapist." Kit sips his beer and looks out over the lake.

Holy Shit, who does that? "Jesus Kit." Husband finally chimes in. Men don't like this kind of talk. *I'm going to be more like a man.*

"Honestly, it got to the point where I did not even like her as a person or as the mother of our daughters. She drank all the time and spent so much money shopping. It was ridiculous. But when Dr. Housel told me about the abortion I had to leave her." Kit concludes. " I guess I should have known when she wouldn't wear my grandmother's engagement ring. She said it was too small." Thank god Husband didn't have a small family heirloom that I *had* to wear.

"And she got the breast implants behind my back with my money." Kit is looking at Husband who has huge eyes and his mouth open. Boys love boobs.

"Had you two already discussed separating?" I ask. *She's a thief and a liar. Kitty is crazy!*

"Yes, so she must of figured she'd need them to land her next sucker." I can tell Kit is exhausted from the whole ordeal.

"Well let's change the subject. We can talk about fun stuff. Can I set you up with someone?" I ask thinking Kit with exotic Allegra might be really cute.

Kit laughs, hard. "Yeah, go for it. At this point who wants a 40 year old with four daughters!" Kit isn't being serious. Even I would go out with him if I didn't have adorable Husband. I guess Kitty and I have the same taste in men. *Yuck!*

Kit leaves shortly after dinner. I walked him to the door. He thanked me and gave me a hug that lasts too long. I totally understand. He is going through a lot. I go back to the living room and sit on Husband's lap. "Are Kitty and I alike?" I ask wondering why we both were with Duncan. That does happen. Some girls just attract the same men and are always going to be competitive with one another. No wonder she resents me so much.

"No honey, Kitty is egotistical and maniacal. You, my dear, are materialistic and spoiled!" Husband kisses me on the shoulder. It's closest to his mouth.

I jump up. "Let's listen to our song!" I call out to Field and Greye. They love to dance. We dance to "Umbrella," by Rihanna.

"So let the rain poor, I'll be all you need and more. When the sun shines we'll shine together. I told you I'd be here forever. Said I'd always be your friend. Took an oath and I'm sticking with it till the end. But now that it's raining more than ever know we'll still have each other, under my umbrella." Rihanna blares on the Bose.

"Ella, ella, ella, eh, eh, eh," Greye sings along as we dance in a circle holding hands. "It's raining. Lean into to me. It's pouring. You can fall into to me." Rihanna sings.

I am getting choked up. I am the umbrella for my boys and Husband. And I am their Cinderella. Who needs an official title? I am Husband's princess and he's my prince. We may not have Ten million dollars but we have love. All I have ever wanted is to be worshiped by a man. And now I'm worshiped by three. Wow! Dreams really do come true in a major way.

Envy, hate and evil ruin not only your looks but also your life. Kitty is jealous of me. I have it all and she wants that too. I can't hate her for being an SC. That would be self-loathing. Which would be bad for my complexion. I was being one too. I just thought she had married into all this money. It blinded me. I thought she had it all. She didn't. I wanted to be like her but what she was, was awful. I cannot be fulfilled wanting to be someone else. I learned that I have to love myself. Kitty failed. I found true happiness. I am the real deal. I was distracted by all her jewelry. Imitation is the highest form of flattery. She copied my citrine after all. I should have known she had a publicist. I was one for crying out loud! She was busy hating me and talking about me behind my back. Well, the more people talk about you the more fabulous you are!

Chapter XXXX

How To Not Have Flat Hair

"It" girls summer in Maine. Allegra's grandmother bought her a house in Kennebunkport, Maine. Allegra does not like summers in Philadelphia. And although she does have to travel for work August is her families self-proclaimed vacation month. Allegra cannot stand how the humidity makes her hair flat so she decided to vacation near the Bush's' estate in Maine. *I want her problems, truly.* Allegra has been begging me to visit. Blue Hill is a few hours north of there. But she keeps promising I will see Jenna and her new husband. Allegra thinks it's ridiculous to drive any further than you have to. Kennebunkport is the first cool town when you cross the state border. Blue Hill is much farther up. What a waste, Allegra wants me to rent near her next summer. We'll see. She is here in June setting up for August. I think Henry has the month of August off too!

"Hello?" I call as I enter her palatial house. It is stunning. It sits up high on a hill over looking the water. It is the largest "cottage" I have ever seen with one of those cool all wood doors.

"Hi!" Allegra shouts from the top of her stairs. She is all wet and wrapped in a towel with her hot pink initials monogrammed onto it. "I'll be right down. Frannie is making lunch."

I greet Frannie in the kitchen and get seltzer water from the fridge. I begin walking through the house. It came furnished. It isn't totally Allegra's taste but it is neat. I love the nautical theme.

During lunch Allegra's love life comes up. "So, I hear Frank is engaged." Allegra smirks. Allegra is wearing silk JM shorts with a coral print. A long sleeved coral cashmere sweater is loose on her bony shoulders. She looks exotic. No humidity here to bother her beautiful golden brown hair.

"How did you hear that?" I ask.

"He told me. He is still calling me all the time. Should I just get new phone numbers?" Allegra would never give up her numbers that she pounded the phone company to give her. They end in 1000. Easy to remember.

"He won't be able to call you once he is married," I hope. "Does Henry know that he still calls you?" Frank needs to disappear. He is a problem in Allegra's life.

"No. I just don't answer the phone when he calls and I'm with Henry. Sometimes I have to turn off my phone or Frank will just keep texting and calling." He's psycho.

I decide to tell Allegra about Duncan. It's over now. Kitty is out of the picture. She can't make me feel guilty anymore. What she did is way worse.

"Shit! Why didn't you tell me that! You never hold out on me." Allegra reprimands.

"I was so sick of the whole situation. Mommie always says 'if you don't want people to find out, don't talk about it to *anyone.*' I wanted it to go away." I conclude.

"You were dead. You were doomed. Of course she was going to try to make your life a living hell. He admitted, in front of both of you, that it was *you* he always liked." Allegra is wide eyed.

"I know. I know." How sad for Kitty.

"Would you ever let me set you up with Kit?" I ask, changing the subject. I have been dying to ask her but knew it would come off better in person.

"No!" Allegra shrieks. *How girly of her*, I think. "I am not raising Kitty's daughters. How odd." She is way more interested than she is acting.

"Fine. Just marinade on it for a while. Don't say no right away. He is a cutie pie and he would be nice to you. Look at what he was putting up with." I rationlize it for Allegra. She would have a good life. "I have a new theory, want to hear it?" I ask.

"Sure," Allegra takes a bite of salad. Fran is a really good cook.

"I think men are attracted to women who are the opposite of them in looks. Kit and Duncan both have blond hair, so does Kitty. Blonds like Brunettes which is why Duncan liked me." I believe this, really. Also men want to marry someone just like their mother. It's true. "So you'll be perfect with Kit, since your hair is technically brown. Albeit light brown you are still Burnett." I finish my new theory.

"Whatever!" Allegra rolls her eyes at me. I'm so MC. "Well then if your right Henry and I are doomed. He has brown hair too." Allegra and Kit sitting in a tree K I S S I N G!

On the way home I listen to Meat Loaf, "Took the words right out my mouth," blares as I drive back to Blue Hill.

Chapter XXXXI

PEOPLE NEVER CHANGE

It is now July 4th weekend, and I've been living in Blue Hill, Maine for four weeks. I have eight more glorious weeks left to be here. Husband is not here yet for the weekend. He has been at home working Monday thru Thursday. We do miss him during the week but it makes it all that much better when he arrives. I can really spoil him. I have really been appreciating all that I have. I am a good person. I am going to heaven with grandmother.

This summer I have decided that the house and myself are going to smell of coconut. Island smell is divine! We only use Hawaiian Tropic sun tan lotion. Neutrogena makes coconut body wash and I found organic coconut shampoo, conditioner and lotion at CVS. Secret makes coconut deodorant. *Could you die!* I also found potpourri and candles for the living room. Everything smells scrumptious. I even put the potpourri in my car. Michael Kors perfume, shimmer lotion and shimmer leg stick go perfectly with coconut. So not only do I smell yummy I am as glittery as my engagement ring. My plan is to wear a lot of white this summer. Very bohemian preppy. My bikini is from J. Crew with my monogram on the boy shorts in brown. I also have an Anne Cole white one piece with a plunging neckline that goes down to my belly button. So risqué! And a white tunic beach cover up from Lands End. I also bought gold hoop earrings. I look as relaxed as I feel. Plus, I've been really well behaved and not watching E! News.

I am taking the boys to the club for fireworks and a picnic. Greye and Field are dressed in matching madras shorts with white long-sleeved Polo shirts and adorable crocs. I am wearing a pair of my Miss Trish's Capri sandals with a little gold frog on them and little diamonds all throughout. Along with little white short shorts and a beautiful ivory Irish knit sweater, my legs are lightly tanned from being here for four weeks. I am walking over to the Club with my two beautiful babies holding my hands, and there is Skyler Scott. I wave, as my two boys run off to play on the beach.

Skyler waves back. She greets me and offers me a glass of wine. Skyler Scott is the type of person that you want to be friends with. Definitely an AT! She has a Pierre Deux diaper bag and matching luggage. Her sons are always wearing matching Vineyard Vines swimsuits and flip-flops. She is just too tempting. She is wearing a casual long sleeves blouse from Molly B and short shorts from Theory, and Goffredo Fantini kitten heels to boot. You can always judge a lady by her clothes. It makes it easier to spot friends. Skyler also grew up outside Philadelphia, but I never knew her because she went to Miss Porter's. Before boarding school she grew up in Chestnut Hill, which is very old-school Philadelphia Prep. Skyler did the Assemblies when she was a debutante. I bet she belongs to the Gulf Mills Golf Club. Skyler's family owns in Blue Hill. She is the fourth generation. Her house, named The Great Scott, is one of the biggest and most beautiful in all of Blue Hill. The sign out front is a ship with all the family names engraved in order of generation. Yes, she is related to the famed Hope Montgomery Scott from the movie "Philadelphia Story." Skyler is on the red team. I like her. That's a bad sign, as I am not a good judge of character. Colby always says I like the crazies. You know, why buy a new wardrobe when you can just make new friends! *Maybe I'll start hanging out in Chestnut Hill.*

"Hi," I say smiling. "How are you?"

"Great! How do the boys like Blue Hill?" Skler's blond hair is shiny. And she has lots of diamond bands stacked on her right hand. Trés chic!

"They love it." We all do.

Skyler says, "I've been thinking about you, and I think you would be perfect for this committee I am putting together for The Local Hospital."

My new theory about ATs, SCs and Ubs is: You don't have to kiss ass, or kill them with kindness. Take the high road and be yourself. *See how smart I am now?* I still want Roberto Coin jewelry, but I'm a kinder person. Things make me happy but so does love, forgiveness, change, acceptance and gratitude.

With a twinkle in my eye I say, "Absolutely, tell me everything about it." *I just can't help myself.* A leopard never changes its spots!

Words to live by:

"Nobody can make you feel inferior without your permission," Eleanor Roosevelt.

The moral of the story is this. And I hope you can learn from my experience and not the hard way. Everyone is doing his or her best to get by in this world. SCs are from out of town and they have new money. They did not grow up in a secure setting. Kitty judged me; at least I lived in Radnor. They are operating in a place of fear. SCs have something terrible going on in their life. My policy is to avoid SCs.

"It" girls are friendly and fun. They want the world to be a swell place to live just like you and me .

P.S. I got asked to be on the Program Book Committee (remember the year book) for the 150th anniversary of The Academy Ball. I win! That's way more prestigious than the silly old opera. And this year the guest speaker is better than Oscar. It's Prince Charles! I might get to actually meet a prince. A real live prince. I hope he brings Harry. I think those boys are so cute! So even though Kitty talked behind my back no one was listening. I must have made quite the impression at the photo shoot. Mommie's reaction was typical, she said, "Of course they asked you. You are *my* daughter, after all."

Kitty

Kitty became best friends with the sales girl at Knit Wit. That's where Kitty worked after the divorce. It was so strange. I hear they spent the whole summer together. She is, like, 24: way inappropriate. At first everyone thought that because Kitty is going through a divorce she was trying to relive her youth. It isn't as if any of her other friends could go out every night till all hours dancing at D'Angelo's. True to SC form, Kitty had real motivation. It turns out this naïve girl has a father who had just built the new library at Penn (not actually, he donated the money). I must say I am impressed with Kitty's research abilities. Apparently the girl not only introduced Kitty to her father, but it did not even dawn on her that it was strange when Kitty was invited, last minute, to her brother's wedding. It turned out that he brought Kitty even though his wife was there. He and Kitty had a torrid romance, and he is now leaving his wife for Kitty. I think that poor 24-year-old grew up fast from that. Needless to say, they are no longer friends. I don't think Kitty cares. She got an eight-carat diamond to boot. A real one. *Damn! Now I need a bigger ring!* Kitty takes being an SC to a new level. I guess her new breasts came in handy. She got herself pregnant right away so that poor man had to marry her. I bet she will try to be friends with Pippa now.

Allegra decided if Divorce is the new "It" trend that she would start a newer one. If Tamara Mellon can raise her daughter and run Jimmy Choo, why even bother getting married? Allegra decided that never getting married was going to be the new "It" trend, and she will be the leader. She can live with someone forever like Goldie and Kurt or she can just do it all on her own with or without children. Frank is finally getting married and has stopped harassing her. Henry didn't work out either. I am hoping she runs into Kit when she returns from Maine. Mimi is thinking of seconding the trend. She called off the wedding. Men just aren't worth the aggravation of divorcing.

Colby's going into marital therapy with her husband. Her parents told her not to worry about the house. She will get to keep it either way. They had her husband sign a pre-nup without telling her. Maybe that's why her husband is being so nasty. Dermatologists make a lot more money than General Practitioners.

Pippa is going to find out what it's really like to be a mother. She is expecting and due in February! Britta is so excited her brother is having another baby she offered to throw the baby shower. Pippa is so flattered that they are actually getting along and being nice to one another. Pippa finally bought Britta's children presents. Silver frames from Tiffany & Co. with a picture of the ultra sound in it. The best part is Britta and Pippa are co-chairing PAS together next year.

The End

Acknowledgements

To my very first editors: My stepmother Connie and Aunt Loretta, thank you. To my Father whose idea this was in the first place, of course. To my Mother, if you hadn't put me white glove dancing class, etiquette school, debutante teas etc. I probably wouldn't have had anything to write about. For my Nana and PopPop, thank you for believing in me. To my loving husband, Rick, who supported me throughout our entire married life. Thank you for letting me explore yet another of my whims. To my sons Greye and Wyn who push me everyday to be a better person without even realizing it. For teaching me who I want to be when I grow up, as we grow together. I hope you love someday the way I love you little pieces of heaven on earth. You are the loves of Mommies life!

Printed in the United States
131034LV00001B/6/P

9 781438 933610